# True Colors

## 1004 Days as a Prisoner of War

by

**James Thompson**

# True Colors

## 1004 Days as a Prisoner of War

by

## James Thompson

Ashley Books, Inc.
Port Washington, N. Y. 11050

TRUE COLORS:1004 DAYS AS A PRISONER OF WAR
Copyright©1989 by James Thompson.

Library of Congress Number:88-39295
ISBN:0-87949-282-1

ASHLEY BOOKS, INC/*Publishers*
Port Washington, New York 11050

Printed In The United States of America
First Edition

9 8 7 6 5 4 3 2 1

All rights reserved, including the right to reproduce this book or portions thereof in any form without permission in writing from the publisher. Address all inquiries to ASHLEY BOOKS, INC., 30 Main Street, Port Washington, New York 11050.

Library of Congress Cataloging in Publication Data:
Thompson, James 1917-
  [Camp 5]
  True colors:1004 days as a prisoner of war / by James Thompson.
     p. cm.
  Reprint. Originally published:Camp 5, Laguna Beach, Ca:Voyager Press, 1981.
  ISBN 987949-282-1
  1. Korean War, 1950-1953--Personal narratives,
     American. 2. Thompson, James, 1917-.
  3. Afro-American soldiers--Biography. 4.Korean War, 1950-1953--Prisoners and prisons,North Korean. 5.Prisoners of war--United States. 6. Prisoners of war: Korea (North) I. Title.
   [DS921.6.T47 1989]                    88-39295
     951.9'042--dc19                         CIP

# Contents

| | |
|---|---|
| Acknowledgments | vii |
| | |
| Foreword | ix |
| —The Honorable Charles E. Rangel, U.S. Congressman | xi |
| —Felix Seldon, U.S. Army Lieutenant Colonel, (Ret.) | xiv |
| —Dolores E. Carmichael, President, Consultant Services | xvi |
| —Bob Greer, U.S. Army Captain, (Ret.) | xix |
| —John C. Fralish, U.S. Army Colonel, (Ret.) | xxi |
| | |
| About James Thompson | xxv |
| | |
| Introduction | xxvii |
| | |
| Chapter 1 — Capture | 11 |
| Chapter 2 — 400 Miles at 40 Below | 20 |
| Chapter 3 — Two Hours on Ice | 29 |
| Chapter 4 — Propaganda Victims | 44 |
| Chapter 5 — Forced Study | 63 |
| Chapter 6 — Brainwashing | 71 |
| Chapter 7 — Camp Elections | 79 |
| Chapter 8 — Solitary Confinement | 84 |
| Chapter 9 — An Uppity Smart-Ass | 93 |
| Chapter 10 — Lice Plague | 105 |
| Chapter 11 — Escape Fizzled | 112 |
| Chapter 12 — More Dashed Hopes | 121 |
| Chapter 13 — "Hank", From Back Home | 125 |
| Chapter 14 — Peace Talks Underway | 128 |
| Chapter 15 — "Dig!" "You Dig Your Grave" | 133 |
| Afterword | 142 |

# Acknowledgments

I am forever grateful to my Aunt Sallie, who was always available for guidance from my birth until her death. It was at her insistence I go to church and sit in the front seat she had so richly earned through long years of service.

To my daughter, Clarissa, who was born after my return from Korea. Her undying belief I had a story to tell and that her daddy would be the best person to tell it, because he lived it. Too bad she is not living to read *True Colors*.

To my wife, Florence, who down through the years endured hardships, criticism and loss of friends. She continued to have faith that I would return. I am keenly aware this was not easy. Thank you.

To Mrs. Dolores Carmichael, who took reins in the middle of a crisis. Without her long hours of hard work, attention to duty, *True Colors* would not have made it to the publisher.

# Foreword

> Out, out brief candle!
> Life's but a walking shadow, a poor player
> That struts and frets his hour upon the stage
> And then is heard no more: it is a tale
> Told by an idiot, full of sound and fury,
> Signifying nothing.
> Macbeth, Act V, Scene 5

Recognizing these truths which Macbeth cried out, I, as an American, can fully understand and do applaud the author of *True Colors*. This fellow American detained as a prisoner of war during the Korean Conflict for 1004 days, now shares the undeniable, painful and historical account of his ordeal.

To me, *True Colors* is not intended to present a study of blacks reaction and motivation in a psychological and physiological sense while in captivity but as a significant kaleidoscope of truths during an experience of war shared with you by a dedicated, patriotic American who happens to be black. I feel compelled to help preserve this fragment of black contribution to these United States so it does not become a walking shadow snuffed out like the light from a brief candle.

Notably, *True Colors* has an equally broader purpose. Not only does this book reveal a story of black life nobody else has dared to tell, it also graphically details truths about blacks and whites agonizing in captivity; about P.O.W. treatment by third-world captors being color-blind; and discredits myths that blacks received preferential treatment from non-white captors.

This documentary brings to the reader some very ugly details about the North Korean and Chinese communist captors and outlines the brain-washing visions they left with their prisoners, i.e., there would be a high use of drugs in the American educational institutions; that drugs would lead to the eventual overthrow of America; plus gives a chronological account of how the communist pitted one against the other . . . black against black . . . black against white . . . white against white. To them we were all the enemy. Nothing was sacred, nothing was spared.

There is no doubt in my mind that *True Colors* was also written as a testament to the men and women who leave their homes to fight and die in strange lands. Hopefully James Thompson's works will help people to better understand the prisoner of war's confrontation with life and death every minute, every hour, every day. I do know the author shares with you the innermost secrets, anxieties and passions that grow and perish in the deepest part of ourselves.

LET US NOT FORGET that a country is no stronger than its weakest link, and it starts with people and ends with people. The United States will not survive should we fail to cause harmony among our people. Despite injustices, blacks and other minorities continue to fight and die for this country. This is a fact of life that must and will continue. Obstacles of prejudice will not arbitrarily be removed. All of us must continue the fight, within the Constitution, to right the injustices and erase vestiges of racism and discrimination.

Let us not permit the spirit of *True Colors*, full of sound and

fury, signify nothing, or forget the courage of the "Forgotten 33".
—Charles Rangel, U.S. Congressman,
16th Congressional District, N.Y.
Fellow Member of United States Army
2nd Infantry Division
(This unit is still in Korea, keeping the peace.)

Just as the longest journey begins with but a single step, James Thompson's journey began the day of capture.

Just as most journeys undertaken by thoughtful, civilized men are well planned and mapped to conclusion, James Thompson's journey started in chaos, proceeded through uncertainty and ended at a bittersweet destination.

The readers are drawn by the author's true life experience through a journey of 1004 days of terror, helplessness, deprivation, courage and survival.

In a man's life there can be few experiences worse than having to look down the barrel of an enemy's weapon, knowing full well that only a short time ago you were doing everything in your power to destroy his existence. James Thompson tells how he survived.

Having had the privilege of knowing the author over years, it is sometimes hard to imagine this fatherly mannered, highly intelligent, truly good man has been subjected to such terror.

In *True Colors* we learn about an enemy who in most cases chooses not to kill, but to mentally conquer. James Thompson

# True Colors

tells a story about himself and about the civilized, courageous American men placed in a situation and manipulated by others.

In *True Colors* we learn about captors equipped with mind and body altering techniques developed over centuries.

In *True Colors* the techniques geared to divide, create suspicion, and cause the man, the group, the race and the nation to turn on itself and self-destruct are revealed.

James Thompson, the man, the brave, the proud United States Army Sergeant Major, the black American withstood all his captors could give. He withstood the shame of captivity and has withstood the shame he felt for the *ignorance* of some of his fellow countrymen upon returning to freedom in his own land.

Only the heart and mind of each reader will draw the true meaning of this saga.

—Felix Seldon
United States Army Lieutenant Colonel (Ret.)

Detroit Diesel Allison
General Motors Corporation
Senior Staff Assistant

*James Thompson, author of* True Colors *is an "eternal jewel" in America's Crown that will shine forever, and ever as a symbol of patriotism, struggle, endurance and survival for all Americans and mankind to see.*

    To know James Thompson, author of *True Colors*, and work closely with him over a period of years, I say with absolute confidence whatever perspective one uses to examine the man, the conclusion must be . . . James Thompson is unique.

    I am sure historians will also find this true as they gather material for the annals of history about this author's most honorable 27 years of service in the United States Armed Forces, the first black noncommissioned officer to reach the high rank of Command Sergeant Major. However, regardless of the fact Thompson has wall to wall credentials, commendations, medals and whatever else is given to deserving people, one would have trouble trying to obtain such information directly from Thompson, for he is a very humble and unassuming person.

    My credentials as a literary critic are nonexistent, therefore,

I offer an insight of the man himself from what is called empathy and my unqualified assessment of his work.

*True Colors* is a conscience disturbing documentary that will definitely have different meaning for everyone who reads this author's work. Within its pages, many readers may find a reason to check their priorities and goals, and start self-examination of conscience regarding how they relate to fellow human beings, especially those of us who might think, look, act or come from different backgrounds. Since we live in a global, interracial society, it is very important to understand the survival plight of others and the differentiation of people and cultures. *Ignorance* is costly.

In reading the author's documentary, I am ever mindful of being placed in St. Joseph Orphanage, Green Bay, Wisconsin at age two. The orphan home was a secluded institution where: Extreme poverty was better than nothing; Maximum discipline was the prime mechanism used by a dozen nuns to effectively control 1000 unwanted youngsters; Your 4th birthday meant day in, day out work assignments instead of cake and candles; Formal education ended at age twelve or after grade six, whichever came first. A profound indifference to *survival* was a constant preoccupation.

Still not being wanted by anyone, this waif was placed in the care of Sisters of Charity Cloister Convent (Green Bay) where self-denial, hard work and charity (beyond Webster's definition) was the way of life.

My introduction to the outside world came at 21. A lone *white* female with no money family or friend was indeed a test of self-confidence. Apprehension and *ignorance* about a world, people and cultures proved to be very costly. My survival depended on many of those ingrained attributes (self-discipline, self-denial, compassion, understanding and love for all people) the Sisters of Charity ingrained in my personality—true, even today.

However, because there still remains that inner doubt of self-worth, my unconscious reaction to people is to mentally put them in categories of: "Takers"; "Givers"; "Superficial Givers"; "Liars"; "Phonies". Doing this is sometimes considered unjust, but it has been my survival mechanism. James Thompson, in my opinion, is a "Giver" and a survivor.

Thompson writes of his imprisonment, suffering, lack of food, self-discipline, little hope of survival, and apprehension about the future. I believe the years leading up to this period in his life (also filled with adversity) molded his compassionate understanding of people and enabled him to survive with dignity. Being born with a different skin color than his, will never allow me to know the full extent of his suffering, nor will it ever give complete confidence one can. But growing up the hard way does help.

I do know Thompson's entire life is an open book with lessons in Courage; Humility; Respect and love for God, country and humanity. He is the type of person who always thinks of others before self and never says "No" to anyone in need.

*True Colors* is untold history made accessible to the public with a message bound to test our true colors. We definitely need more Thompsons. He is my kind of hero.

>—Dolores E. Carmichael
>President, Management Consultant Services
>Citizens for Better Government
>Executive Board of Directors

# True Colors

This unparalleled, magnificent story reveals a black soldier's appalling experience of survival for about three years in a prisoner of war camp during a war that was not a war, the Korean Conflict. As I read and re-read the advanced drafts of these vivid, horrifying, intimidating truths, I found myself, a Korea and Vietnam veteran, a veteran of more than 27 years, not for the first time, repeatedly and privately asking myself: "How would I have carried the "TWO STICKS?" Without having endured an internment filled with such callous, inhuman, agonizing, and excruciating experiences, I cannot honestly say.

Jim's frank and intimate confessions and unanswered truths of this side of black military history, cannot and must not be ignored, anymore than blacks can turn their backs on yesterday's deprivations, on today's struggles, on tomorrow's aspirations. The legacy of our military blacks, who so suffered, who so fought, and who so died, enables us to improve upon the contemporary standards of living that we now enjoy. Other unidentified exploits of faceless Jim Thompson's have yet to tell their stories, have yet to make their voices heard. *My God!!! What a shame.*

Who is this black man? Who is this retired Sergeant Master Major James Thompson, RA 36 101 834, U.S. Army? Well hear this. His distinguished military profile reveals that he was born in Bacum, Arkansas. Pardon my ignorance, but where in the hell is that? And, finally, he was inducted into the U.S. Army at Fort Wayne, Detroit, Michigan. Our personal association dates back to 1949, and to his friends and family he is known as Jim, Thompson, Top Kick, or Sergeant Major Thompson. Jim is a very honorable, private, unassuming and humble person. Even to know him personally, you would not receive any utterances from him that he had been received more than once at the White House by the President of the United States. However, you would quickly become impressed by the facts that he is a genuine and dedicated family man, has high standards and ideals, conducts himself gentlemanly, and meets all the attributes of having been a soldier's soldier. But, what about Jim's meager beginning? In other words, what about his famial roots? Aren't these the biological and moral fibers that make up the person? All throughout his ordeal, Jim's infinite strength was achieved by an iconic symbolization that society imposes upon blacks, that is the need for blacks to carry "Two Sticks," while others need carry only one. By his innate ability to relate to this symbolization, he survived the imposed exile that surely must have galled and traumatized his sensitive spirit.

For many readers, Jim's refusal to succumb to extraordinary cruelty by his captors may be an unbelievable feat. However, knowing him as I do, and you will know him too by reading this book, you will understand when I say: "Today, Jim still gives of himself to the greatest cause that he perceives as being the most important, America."

*Bob Greer, US Army Retired Captain*
*Project Officer, Bell Telephone Company*
*Detroit, Michigan*

# True Colors

(Note: Retired Army Colonel John C. Fralish was Commander of the 503rd Fire Direction Center in North Korea. He was engaged in the battle during which James Thompson was captured. The Colonel's responsibility was to direct the artillery fire of Thompson's units. In other words, his job was to pinpoint the range and direction of the enemy and order fire from Thompson's artillery batteries. It must also be stated that Colonel Fralish had trained the black battery units of the 503rd at Fort Lewis, Washington. The black servicemen regarded Fralish as "hard nosed, tough, no-nonsense, but fair." They respected his leadership and were quite apprehensive when, suddenly, just before departing for Korea, the Army command reassigned Fralish, sending another white officer to replace him.

During repeated actions in Korea, the black artillery soldiers became increasingly suspicious of the competency of the newly assigned white officer and openly sought the return of Fralish. Some blacks theorized that it was the same old story, "assign the incompetent white officers to blacks and the competent white officers to the white units . . ."

The newly assigned white officer was finally removed

*when he mistakenly ordered the artillery units to fire in the direction of a U.S. general's quarters. Fortunately, the general was not in at the time. That led to the quick reassignment of the officer and the return of Fralish to the black units.*

*Years after the war, many of the black veterans formed an organization called the Indianhead Association. Just prior to their first annual convention, they decided to invite all of the white officers with whom they had contact while in Korea. Many suspected that if any showed up it would no doubt be Fralish. And, indeed, he did and has been attending ever since. Many Indianhead members strongly believe that Fralish should have been awarded the Medal of Honor because of his heroics in Korea. Others suspect that because he had commanded black units he was not taken seriously.*

*The following letter,* unedited, *was forwarded to Thompson just prior to publication of this documentary. It is published here with the permission of Colonel Fralish.*

Dear Sergeant Major Thompson:

I know that you are planning to have your book regarding our involvement in the Korean War published soon. I really want to get one of your books as soon as it is available. I know it is going to be a wonderful book, and it is important to help so many Americans realize how we were involved in the Korean War.

We are fortunate that as many of us, who are now members of the Indianhead Association, have been able to survive and to get together each year to attend our Indianhead Association reunion. I am so happy that I was able to help so many of us survive during that terrible fight we were involved in.

I am sure that you realize that I have reported in my list of so many things that happened on November 30, 1950 (my birthday) when we were surrounded by five divisions of Chinese in the Battle of the Caongchon River, including what happened to you when we were going up over the mountain and all of a sudden we were receiving a heavy fire and you were injured. As you remember, I talked with you and you told me you were "all right," but, later, when the sun came up and I looked around to see if anyone had been killed or captured, I found that you were no longer with us.

I prayed to God that you and the other soldiers who also were no longer with us would survive. I never knew whether you had survived until we got together in the Indianhead Association, which was great! And I thanked our God!

When I receive your book, I know it will include your autograph, which will be wonderful.!

I am sure that you remember that when the 503rd FA Battalion had gotten onto the road to go south, following the other units of the 2nd Infantry Division, and all of a sudden the Chinese destroyed most all of "B" Battery just ahead of me, we had a terrible situation in trying to survive. One of the main problems was that neither our commander nor any of the commanders of the battalions that were behind us would make a decision about what we could do to survive. As the Chinese began to come closer to us and were firing machine guns, mortars, bazookas, etc., at us from the ridges on both sides of the roads and the firing was exploding all around us, it was obvious that we had to describe how to survive, and I decided I had to make the decisions and take command, which I did!

I got the Flak Wagons brought up to help us get moving by firing heavily at the Chinese, which they did. Within about thirty minutes after I got the Flak Wagons and trucks going, we were able to continue to move South. If I had not taken command and given orders, and if our soldiers had not done what I ordered them to do, none of us would have survived.

My estimate of how many Chinese soldiers we killed is about one thousand. Our members of the 503rd FA Battalion knew that I had trained them at Fort Lewis, Washington, and they had become the best unit of all black soldiers (except about one half of the officers in the 503rd FA Battalion were white) in the U.S. Army, as reported by our Commander (Brig. General Haynes). He had reported to the Congressmen who were investigating the black units in the Korean War (about a month before) that the 503rd FA Battalion was 100% as good as the white units.

So when I took command and started giving orders, everyone who was with us immediately did just what I ordered them to do. Everyone started helping; moving the trucks; loading the wounded soldiers in them; firing back at the Chinese and keeping them from capturing or killing all of us.

I had recommended to all of the Battalion commanders who were with us that we should go back north and turn left and go west on the road that we had passed before (about 5 miles north) and go south on the road which other units, including the 25th Infantry Division, had already gone south with no problem.

Thank God that we are able to be members of our Indianhead Association and able to attend our annual reunions.

Sincerely,

Col. John C. Fralish
USA Ret.

# About James Thompson

James Thompson, author of *True Colors,* vowed years ago to write a book based on his Prisoner of War experience as seen from the perspective of a black who was actually there. He was among the last to be released from communist North Korea and Chinese captivity, long after the cessation of hostilities.

Thompson, the oldest of three children, grew up in Bacum, Arkansas on a farm owned by his parents, Daniel and Gussie Thompson.

After serving in the C.C.C. (Civilian Conservation Corps), Thompson was inducted in the Armed Forces in 1941 from Detroit, Michigan. He married Florence Frey, a school teacher from Weir, Kansas. They had one child, Clarissa (now deceased). He attended Oakland University, Rochester, Michigan and Northwood Institute, Midland, Michigan.

Command Sergeant Major Thompson, United States Army (Retired), meritoriously served on active duty for 27 years. He is a veteran of W.W. II, The Korean Conflict, and Vietnam. Thompson received the Purple Heart for wounds inflicted by the enemy during the Korean Conflict, which resulted in his capture.

Thompson is living testimony to some historic events of the

past half century. In addition to combat, he participated in the 6th Atomic Nuclear Blast at Yucca Flats, Nevada in 1955 and the final countdown in the Cuban Missle Crisis during the Kennedy Administration in 1962.

James Thompson retired as Command Sergeant Major in November 1967 from the United States Army Tank Automotive Command, Warren, Michigan and is still a resident of Detroit. He recently completed a two-year appointment by Michigan Governor James J. Blanchard on the Commission of Economic and Social Opportunity. Thompson presented a plan to the Committee on White House Conference on Balanced Growth and Economic Development and received a citation from President James Carter. He wrote and the Department of Defense approved the first Black Military History for the Detroit Board of Education, which is now taught in all public high schools.

Thompson remains active in city, state and national politics besides being on the lecture circuit addressing the consequences of wars, communism and drugs. He is a member of the Indianhead (quasi-military) Association; Optimist International Service Club; Treasurer of Citizens for Better Government (Political Action Committee) and President of Detroit-Metro Contracting Corporation and is currently working on his next book.

Readers of Thompson's works will not only find him to be more than a typical middle American, they will also find him to be a unique man. The valor, along with the historical and political perspective related by Thompson in *True Colors,* is now a part of America's history . . . so is James Thompson.

# Introduction

I am now totally convinced, given the right set of circumstances, a man can be reduced to something he himself cannot easily recognize. I fully understood this after becoming a prisoner of war in North Korea.

A simple, church going, God fearing Christian, I would never have imagined I could ever steal, cheat, lie and even enjoy the very idea of killing another man. I simply never thought anyone could force me to become overwhelmed by a preoccupation of hate . . . but, it happened.

While confined by the Chinese in North Korea from December 1, 1950 until September 3, 1953, I became almost demonic in my quest to survive. There is nothing pretty or fancy about one's lifestyle when faced with the stark reality of death.

To a person casually reading this discourse in the comfort of one's living room with a cold beer nearby, it may be difficult to understand the raw fanaticism associated with the will to live. I can quite easily understand this indifference.

However, if a person who hates your guts becomes enraged with anger and places a loaded revolver to your head and cocks it, you better appreciate the will to survive. You will also understand the depths to which you can sink in order to accomplish this.

Being born in Bacum, Arkansas and living in Detroit, Michigan, I had little experience with people of Chinese ancestry before I entered the Korean Conflict. Those I had casually spoken to were friendly enough, in fact, real nice and courteous.

I had no way of knowing people could still be nice and friendly while sticking a garden hose on full blast down your throat. However, after three years in a North Korean prisoner of war camp, I understood. Make no mistake, I have nothing against the North Korean or Chinese people, even to this day. They were trapped by the same insane war environment as I.

Another appreciation I now have is for the mystery and power of the human mind. It can be a beautiful survival tool. Then again, that same magnificent mind can be effectively used against you by those schooled in the art of mind altering.

The Chinese were also quite adept at planting seeds of racial discord among black and white prisoners. They would orchestrate interrogation sessions designed to create strife among the prisoners. As an example, after rather intense and sometimes brutal sessions with white prisoners, the instructors would set up a makeshift kitchen in the interrogation room and then bring in black prisoners. While this was going on, cooks with aprons would dash in and out of the room, in full view of the white prisoners.

The smell of beef and pork was apparent. It didn't matter that only the Korean interrogators ate. What did matter was the impression we HAD eaten and were cooperating with the enemy. It planted the suspicion. The traditional apprehension between black and white soldiers would do the rest, and the captors knew it.

No matter how we explained to our fellow white prisoners, one could tell they were still suspicious. In fact, these very acts later sparked charges that many of the black prisoners collaborated with the enemy.

Keep in mind that in addition to the basic concerns of food, warm shelter, freedom from beatings, and possible just outright murder, we were all continually aware of the subtle psychological warfare being waged against us daily. The more immediate fear was pain and death. However, the longest lasting agony may well have been the psychological impact, especially for those of us who came back to face later charges of collaborating with the enemy.

To some extent this book is, in part, devoted to correcting that perception. Many of my colleagues have urged me to just dismiss the entire ordeal as just another incident in an unfortunate war that should never have happened.

I thought about it for awhile and even agreed I could perhaps forget sleeping on a bed of lice, spending hours cracking them in order to survive. Thought about forgetting how I was forced to stand barefooted in sub zero temperatures or having my skin ripped repeatedly by the butt of a rifle. I could even ignore the kicks to my groin. Maybe forget the many cold hours spent in a cramped, rat-infested isolation chamber. I could quite possibly forget the starvation, the dysentery and the many near fatal illnesses prompted more by neglect and exposure than anything. I could also forget the indignity and the demeaning lifestyle forced on me by my captors.

But, what I can not and will not dismiss as "just another war story" is the humiliation some of us suffered at the hands of our own government after we were released. To humiliate us, then dismiss us as non-entities, *will not be ignored.*

Lest some interpret my concern as bitterness, please understand that these experiences and the war ended years ago. What has remained are the vivid memories of a story never told to the American public who, at one time, were led to believe some of us were anything but loyal and dedicated men in uniform. This motivates the book, *True Colors* . . . not the intense bitterness one may perceive. To say I am free of all bitterness would be untrue, some will remain forever.

It appeared we had no story . . . only that told by others who drew their own conclusions.

One thing every black man in a white man's world never, never forgets is that he must be the best to succeed and must be well above any and all improprieties. This was not even forgotten while in the Chinese prison camp, some 400 miles north of Pyongyang, the capitol of North Korea. It was just an additional cross to bear in the daily, unreal struggle for survival.

Of all the memories of that camp, the most treasured are my friends, such as, Doc Frazier and Bill Lillis, who just happen to be caucasian. Speaking of Bill, our families became very close. We visited over-seas and always kept in touch. I was the only ex-P.O.W. to attend his funeral. It's a damn shame we must get captured 5000 miles from America to find out we need each other for survival.

I still think of "Bop Daddy" occasionally. "Bop Daddy" was the name we gave to the camp commander because he was a bonafide narcissist. The man was in love with himself and his curly locks.

"Bop Daddy" was a study in contradiction. For the most part he was polite, friendly, smiled a lot and remained meticulously dressed. But, make no mistake, he could turn brutal without notice, as many of us learned. An apparent karate expert, his well-orchestrated kicks to the groin, ribs, stomach and chin will not soon be forgotten by this writer. How a man could administer such punishment and still pause long enough to brush his hair is amusing to me, even now when I tell my friends about him. Not so in 1951, nothing was funny then.

There are other carry-overs from those three years in a North Korean prison. Everytime I feel an itch on my scalp I think of LICE. Not that I have them now, but while in camp lice were a major problem. Our heads and the inside seams of our clothing, for some reason, appeared especially vulnerable, though other body parts were not immune. After a while every body itch was associated with LICE.

# True Colors

Unlike a civilian prison, where one normally has some fix on a release date, there is no such certainty in a war compound. You have no idea whether the agony you are enduring will be over by the next year or in twenty. Each Christmas you play games with yourself, believing by next Christmas you will be home. After three years, you begin to resign yourself to the long haul and intensify your efforts at survival.

I never shall forget the time when a group of us saw a camp guard drop some meat on the floor. We all wanted so badly to pounce like dogs and lap up that pork. Being ashamed was the most remote thing in our minds. We were desperate in a hopeless situation and knew it. Pride and hunger never mixed.

As a rule, depending on overall camp conditions and the treatment given, you soon develop low self-esteem. You care less about shaving and general body appearance. Your appearance takes a back seat to basic day-to-day survival. To prevent major outbreaks of disease we begged for medicine, usually receiving it as a reward, not as a necessity. As a consequence, you damn near had to make the camp authorities feel superior by doing a thousand little demeaning things. What was left of you after a few months resembled your original self only slightly.

Stress and bad nerves quickly begin to play hell with your attempts at staying conversant with reality. Keep in mind, the men who had the guns received a good night's sleep. They were generally well fed and therefore up to the challenge of each morning. We, the prisoners, were only glad we saw the morning, whatever it had in store. To be true, some men mentally and physically gave up. That thought never really entered my mind. Being black in America had taught me years earlier that surviving would be a lifetime ordeal. The places and faces changed, but the determination remained.

This is not to suggest. I was some kind of hero, because I was not. At best, I was a scared man. No ifs, ands or buts about it. I was frightened! But, as most men are inclined to do, I played it off and bore my suffering as best I could. In many respects, we were nonentities, only objects for the captors to push around and brainwash.

Sometimes, as I moved around the compound, I would look at a guard, who, in civilian life, was probably a nonentity, probably a farmer who nobody knew. But, as he swaggered around the camp, we had to cater to his wishes as if he were a damn god, and I resented that more than anything. It's difficult to hold on to one's dignity when a man has a gun pointed at your guts and can pull the trigger at the least bit of provocation.

Sure, the Geneva Convention mandates fair and humane treatment to prisoners of war. But, if you believe this, I will sell you the Brooklyn Bridge with a credit card that has expired. When the lights dim in P.O.W. camps, it's usually open season. There are no Red Cross monitors spending the night.

So, when they ask if you are treated well on the eve of repatriation, you smile and say, "Just fine, thank you. Things couldn't be better unless I was at home." Garbage! Bullshit! Hogwash!

As I reflect back, I also remember how casual the burial details were. Some P.O.W. dies and several of us are assigned to cart him off and bury him. In civilian life we attach a great deal of importance to death, complete with a mourning period and formal funeral. We care, and that's how it should be. But, in a P.O.W. camp, that formality is not there. Sure, you regret the passing, but you are also well aware the next burial detail may well be for you.

As I write this, I am amazed at how easy another outbreak can occur. North and South Korea have had an uneasy truce for years. All hell can break loose at any given moment . . . and this is not a statement to be taken lightly. One of the many skirmishes at the border could get out of hand. That's all it will take. Or, perhaps North Korea decides the Olympic games in South Korea provide a good setting for unleashed acts of terrorism.

Obsessed by my ordeal? Perhaps. Still somewhat crippled by it all? Perhaps. Bitter? Somewhat, but not with any intensity. Grudges still held against the North Koreans and Chinese? No, not at all. As I recall, there were unspeakable acts committed by U.S. Servicemen against civilian refugees in W.W. II, Korea and Vietnam. Then one must remember the Bible says let he who is free of guilt cast the first stone. I certainly cannot.

*FOOTNOTE:* I am fortunate to witness the progress made in our country since those days when segregation in the Armed Forces was as American as apple pie.

The Army now boasts 15 percent of black generals, notwithstanding, that the late President Dwight D. Eisenhower, who served as General of the Armies in Europe and testified as Chief of Staff, before Congress, that integration would not work and a black should never rise above the rank of Adjutant.

Things are so strange. This same individual, as Commander-In-Chief, had to integrate schools in Little Rock, Arkansas and start us on the way to the 1964 Civil Rights Act. What a damn pity the Armed Forces had to lead the way. Any suffering I might have encountered has not been in vain. "GOD BLESS AMERICA."

# 1
# Capture

It's now 1988, I'm retired and quite warm in our modest but comfortable home here in Detroit. I can put on some soft music, hop in bed, and nestle up snugly to my wife, Florence. There is much peace, love and order in this modest house in Detroit on this wintry night in January 1987.

Not so 38 years ago. Then I was with the battle weary remnants of the once proud and cocky 155th Howitzer Battalion. We were freezing our tails off in 20-degree below zero temperatures about 150 miles north of the North Korean capital of Pyongyang. Quite frankly, we had gone there to kick the butts off the North Koreans for invading our friends in South Korea. Months earlier we, to the man, figured this wouldn't take too long and that we'd be back home in time for Christmas turkey. After all, General MacArthur had virtually guaranteed this. That's one reason we didn't bother to bring along any heavy clothing. We simply didn't intend to be up North that long, just long enough to kick their little fancy behinds, teach them a lesson and come on back home a hero. Having fought a real world war against the Germans in France and Germany, Korea wasn't supposed to be any big deal. Just enough "bragging action" to tell the grandchildren about some day. Just a little "muscle flexer" to retain our fighting edge. But, on that cold, damp and weary night in November 1950, we were getting OUR rumps royally kicked by several hundred thousand bugle blowing, shouting, gun blazing Communist Chinese fanatics surrounding us atop mountains. Looking back, that November 29th night now appears unreal, as if it were all imagined. I know now that in a struggle for life and death even a close friend will blow your damn head off in order to save his. In a state of fear, the king and servant both become equals.

The Chinese had us in a complete circle as they rained down rifle and mortar fire with fanatical zeal, all the time blowing those damn bugles. At times the Chinese came so daringly close until our units fired upon each other in the resulting confusion and panic. Nothing in my childhood, not even in segregated Arkansas, prepared me for both the psychological and physical warfare waged by the Communist Chinese. Even to this day I find it difficult to understand how a soldier, in the midst of a blazing battle, could take time out to blow a cotton-picking bugle. But, the Chinese did, and to great effect. The sound of the bugle and the gunfire created a chilling affect. It played total havoc with the nerves. During World War Two the sophisticated Germans didn't have time for this type of nonsense. Perhaps that's why we beat their butts so convincingly. But, the Chinese introduced us to something new, and it helped get the job done.

At various intervals, the shooting and bugle blowing stopped. The mountains surrounding us became quiet. Too quiet! We knew they were there. Probably laughing their little rice-filled heads off at our plight. During these dreaded intervals we stared nervously at those damn mountains, wanting those little bastards up there to get it on, anything to salvage the nerves.

"Come on, ya bunch of Buddah heads," someone whispered in desperation.

"Knock it off," came some voice of authority.

Then, without warning, the mountains exploded again with gunfire, bugle blowing, and fanatical shouting.

"Those cotton suckers are good," I remember murmuring to myself, "damn good."

If one knows anything about the ghetto, then one knows a lot about street language. You won't find it in textbooks. They as hell don't teach it in school. Your parents don't cater to your using it in the home. But, if you are a black guy with any kind of roots, you just manage to pick it up. Since we were primarily an all-black unit, a lot of street talk was going down on that shell-riddened cold night in November, 1950.

"Another long hot load, right up the rear!" someone would blurt as we slammed round after round of artillery fire into those mountains.

"Your mama screwed a bear and got a dog for a child," as still another round made its way into the mountains.

"Do it to 'em like Aunt Fannie did it to Uncle Jack." Another round on its way.

"Like your Uncle Willie did it to his dog."

"And the dog's cat."

"And your mama."

"Tell me you still love me when this one tickles your damn guts."

"Hop onto this one, sweetie pie, it's hot."

"Open yer mouths wide, baby, 'cause here it comes."

"This one's marked 'China express,' baby boy, so run out and catch it 'fore it hurts your mama."

All this chatter, mind you, was done with a rhythmic cadence as if to provide a musical sendoff for each round.

Volley after volley after volley we pounded those mountains. Our shells slammed into enemy positions all through the night and into the early morning hours.

To their everlasting credit, those little bastards perched atop those mountains rammed back down our throats everything we threw at them. We were hopelessly outgunned, outmanned and outmaneuvered. But, we still held our positions. We had been told that at 0800 hours the next morning, November 30th, we would be permitted to evacuate our positions and join the other retreating forces. At 0800 hours, however, new orders came down instructing us to remain in position and continue firing to protect our other retreating forces.

I first realized my own unit was in serious trouble when remnants of the badly beaten and exhausted 38th Infantry were suddenly amongst us. The 38th had penetrated farther than any other unit in the area into North Korea. If they had now retreated back to our positions, that meant there was no one to protect us, the black 155th Howitzer Battalion, when it was time for us to retreat. We were it! And, it was frightening! A slow panic began to evidence itself for the first time.

What was left of the 38th Infantry was a sight I shall never forget. I saw men, barely alive, with arms and legs blown off, blood rushing unchecked through hastily wrapped bandages. Someone had placed a cloth over the stomach of one young infantryman to keep his intestines from coming through a large wound. In pain and crying uncontrollably, companions were only able to pay minimal attention to him due to the confusion of the retreat and the constant bombardment we were receiving from the mountains surrounding us. It was rapidly approaching "protect your own ass time."

Those of us who were told to "hold your positions and keep firing" were in a dilemma. We now knew there was no infantry in front of us to protect our own retreat. Of greater concern, however, was the fact that the big guns that had been in the forward positions were now being pulled back, passing through our positions as they headed toward safety. Units consisting mostly of blacks and Turkish soldiers were still being told to "hold and cover the retreating forces." Our fate became a bit clearer when a ranking officer spoke to us on radio, saying in effect that ". . . if you go down, some damn good soldiers went down." That, in all fairness, was a lot of hogwash. Who in the hell wanted to go down when every soul who could move was trying to get out? As hopeless as the situation had become, we all realized that to leave our positions would mean later charges of desertion. This, to a black military man in 1950, was tantamount to treason.

Things really began to fall apart when some of us observed retreating white officers removing their brass and insignia to protect their rank and identity if caught. If we needed the last bit of confidence kicked out of us, that did it. One ray of hope was our Batallion training officer, who was the Junior Field Grade Officer on the Batallion staff. This guy was super. I had been in communication with him all that day. He was giving orders from one Battery to the other, firing direct fire.

As night fell, we then attempted our own retreat. By now the Chinese had closed all escape routes. They had stopped toying with us and were apparently zeroing in for the kill. The ground all around us was being torn up by more intense enemy fire. I leaped onto a speeding half-track along with several others. Bodies and debris were all over the area. A boy from Battery "C" had his head torn off. We sped by one youngster standing in the middle of the road laughing uncontrollably. He didn't know where he was and we didn't have time to stop and tell him. In retrospect, it's difficult to say whether or not I was afraid. Perhaps "numb" would be a more accurate description.

We had not gone too far in the half-track when a small round of mortar slammed into it, causing the vehicle to veer out of control before overturning. I leaped from the wreckage and dashed wildly toward a nearby ditch. To this day I don't know whether anyone was killed or wounded in that half-track. I would like to say that I went back to examine the wreckage for possible survivors who may have been wounded. However, I recall only that at least two others leaped off with me and ran frantically for their own lives. At that moment in life, it was James Thompson against the world. I didn't give a damn about who else survived.

As I ran blindly, I remember slipping, sliding, falling, and returning to my feet almost in one motion. I have absolutely no recollection of how long or far I ran before sensing this burning sensation in my right leg and what appeared to be two mules kicking me in the head at the same time. I apparently blacked out on my feet because I never remember hitting the ground. Only God knows how long I was out or what happened to me while I was unconscious. I recall awakening from my stupor with a blinding headache and lying on a stretcher. Initially, not too much made sense to me. I did note that a white chaplain was talking with whom I slowly came to realize was a Communist Chinese soldier. There were about fifteen other Americans huddled together and being interrogated by enemy soldiers, some not too politely. There was still a lot of confusion. It sounded as if all the enemy soldiers wanted to talk at once. Without fully understanding what the hell was going on, I do remember just being glad old James Thompson was alive. Didn't matter that the chaplain was surrendering our group. Didn't matter that we were now in the hands of a very crafty enemy. Didn't matter that I might not see Florence again. Didn't even matter that I might spend the rest of my life in a stinking North Korean prisoner of war camp. What mattered at that very moment was that this tall, lean and lanky former Arkansas black farm boy was still alive and kicking. Damn the pain in the leg. Damn the headache. Damn the biting cold. Forget the growing hunger. Jimmy was still among the living.

  The Chinese soldiers had placed me about thirty yards away from the rest of the group. My stretcher was also several yards from a small ditch. I could do one of two things. I could lie there like a damn idiot and patiently await whatever fate was in store. Or, I could simply roll over into the ditch. If they saw me, I could lie like a cotton-pickin' dog and say I accidentally tumbled my butt into the ditch. I opted to take the tumble. Make no mistake, being brave and courageous had nothing to do with my decision. I am not necessarily a brave and courageous man. When a person leaps from a blazing two-story building, bravery has absolutely nothing to do with it. It has everything to do with flames being hot.

# True Colors

As it turned out, the enemy soldiers were so busy mounting their own gear and harrassing the other Americans they had simply ignored me. Something else, I had noticed earlier that I was the only black in the captured group. Perhaps I was not high on their priority list. Or, perhaps they considered my now bandaged leg too tender to make a run on it. Or, better yet, they no doubt considered me too chicken to attempt an escape with them this close. At any rate, they knew nothing about a black Arkansas farm boy's endurance. If I could pick wet cotton all day with the flu, I sure as hell could roll into a damn ditch with a bandaged leg in an attempt to flee a bunch of bastards with guns. What's more, if I had two good legs, I could have probably outrun the group of little midgets, all things being equal. But, they weren't. They had guns and I didn't. I did have one thing going: it was still quite early in the morning and there was a measure of darkness to provide some cover. I also deeply appreciated my God-given black face. So, I was off, into the darkness and into the damn ditch. I had guessed that the ditch was about 3-feet deep. That sucker was every bit 8-feet. I almost broke my goddamn neck. This may sound silly, but when I rolled into that deep ditch, I almost yelled for help.

I made my way to the side of a river. I had no idea where I was. With my sense of direction, I could have been heading for downtown China. I knew I had a map before I passed out. But, it was now gone. I decided the best thing to do was to just stay put awhile, clear my head a bit more, get some type of bearing, make me a plan and begin to work whatever plan I fashioned. I remained on the hill next to the river all the following day, until about 8 p.m. With all that patient waiting and brilliant planning, I still didn't know what the hell I should be doing. I finally decided to do what I should have done an hour after I got there, keep moving down the riverside. The moon was shining brightly. The quietness of the riverside combined with the beauty of the moon painted a most romantic picture for any other time and place. But, this was North Korea and a bunch of little midgets were trying to burn my butt. So, I began a slow trot. Suddenly, a shot crackled out of the darkness. I hit the ground. No more shots. I remained motionless. Still, only the quietness of the riverside. The thought then occurred to me that that big beautiful moon was nothing more than a big flashlight for the bastards out there with guns. I decided to make it away from the open riverside, but another crackle of gunfire, the round coming dangerously close. Then, a large flare. Still another flare. Crackle of gunfire.

"Shit," I recall blurting out of frustration.

I didn't want to admit it, but a slow panic was beginning to set in. I had no idea how many were out there, or if they were trying to amuse themselves with a black boy from the states. The Chinese were artists at getting to the mind. And, quite frankly, they were really screwing around with mine out there on that cold riverside.

This cat and mouse game continued for about three hours. No one would fire until I made a dash. Then, the crackle of gunfire. At one point I could have sworn I heard a little son-of-a-bitch out there laugh. Wasn't sure but certainly sounded like it. Down South when a black passed a ground of whites and everyone laughed, you knew who the joke was on. I got this same feeling out there on the riverside.

Suddenly, a yelling and shouting patrol ran from the hills toward me. I started to run, but at least two shots rang out. The game of cat and mouse was over. They decided to take me and did. Since I realized they could have killed me without much effort. I concluded that they wanted me alive.

After several overnight stays in huts along the way, I was finally returned to the other POWs for the long trek to the prison camp. With all my daring, I had accomplished absolutely nothing, except the satisfaction of knowing that I tried.

A soldier senses a very eerie feeling upon being captured. Sure, you are well aware of the supposedly humane treatment of prisoners mandated by the Geneva Convention. That's a bunch of bull and the average fighting man knows it. You lie on your belly day after day trying to blow the head off some poor bastard a mile away. You try to subject him to every conceivable horror of war imaginable. You burn his crops, destroy his supplies, set ablaze his homes and torture his friends. Then, all of a sudden, that bastard captures you and you have the gall to think he's going to abide by some piece of paper hacked out over vodka, coffee and tea. Bullshit! The son-of-a-bitch is now out for blood. What's more, the bastard never believes he is going to lose the war so why should he fear any future punishment?

The minute you are captured it is then ass-kicking time, and you are not the kicker. I knew it and I braced for the worst. Back in Arkansas in 1950 whites and blacks were not permitted to sit at the same lunch counters. But, in North Korea in December 1950, white and black prisoners of war sat together looking down the same rifle barrel and praying to the same God . . . and no one was heard complaining.

# 2
# 400 Miles at 40 Below

Things that are contiguous in time and place tend to recall each other. If you were stung by a bee while picking berries, you'll think about the damn bee whenever you go berry picking. So it is with that first day of travel after our captivity. I remember it well. There are too many reference points for me to ever forget. I remember how the ice formed on our moustaches, how our breaths froze. It was about 40 degrees below zero. Some of the fellows were wearing light clothing and were paying a severe physical price for this misjudgment. They rubbed their frost-bitten hands together, ran in place, folded their arms, clapped their hands, but all to little avail. There is little a poorly clothed human can do in 40-degree below zero temperatures except suffer, pray, and, eventually, urge death to hurry. One nearly frozen young soldier panicked, ran over to a nearby guard and shouted "Kill me, goddammit!"

The guard never lost his composure as he slowly drew back the butt of his rifle and slammed it into the kid's face. The boy fell immediately, grabbing his face with both hands. As the stricken and now blooded young soldier lay writhing on the cold ground, another rather tall guard kicked him in the side several times before dragging the shouting youngster to the side of the road. There was really no need to shoot him. In less than an hour he no doubt would freeze to death.

We marched that first day until some of the men simply began to give up and just drop. The Chinese guards were remarkable in their coolness while dragging fallen bodies from the path of other weary marchers. There was no emotion. No big thing. Just a job.

At the end of the first night's march, the now unbearably cold weather forced us to pile on top of each other in small groups in order to keep warm. I was slow getting in because of so many people. That was a time you wanted to be on the bottom. In the struggle for life, dignity becomes a spectator, not a participant. We almost fought each other as we jockeyed for a warmer position beneath the pile of squirming bodies.

At one point, while I was slowly jockeying for position in the pile, I heard a guard shout. I thought he was actually calling me back. As I was attempting to obey what I thought was his command, he kicked me. The kick was a glancing blow that landed in my groin. To get some idea of the pain, try slamming a car door on your hand in, say, 10-degree temperature. If you can imagine that agony, consider someone kicking the hell out of you in the groin in 40-degree below zero temperatures. I was stunned and weak as I fell to the ground. Quite frankly, at that moment if the son-of-a-bitch had shot me, I would have kissed him for being humane. God! I hurt! I never before nor since hurt that much.

The next morning, I really began to feel the after effects of that little bastard's kick. If I could find the little runt today I would probably try to sign him as a place-kicking coach with one of the professional football teams. That son-of-a-bitch could kick! I was very sore and stiff. I was hurting deep inside. As I started to march out that morning, I became very weary. My pace began to slow and I began to feel sick all over. I can remember stumbling on a rock; my foot just wouldn't move over that rock. The guards rushed over to me and shouted that I had to keep moving "or else." I had quickly come to learn just what "else" meant. I managed to struggle to my feet and continue on with the rest of the POWs.

After a few hours we came to a frozen lake. After crossing it, we were permitted to rest. As I sat in pain alongside the road, a Turkish POW came over and asked what was wrong. I showed him where I was hurting. The Turks are highly regarded for the artistry of their massages. Their fellow prisoner of war leaned down and grabbed my groin area in his hands. He massaged my groin until I was able to walk without the previous pain. The Turkish soldiers, God bless them, eventually tried to administer to as many of the other POWs as possible, massaging their legs, feet, ankles, necks. I shall never forget their compassion for others during a time when personal survival was the order of the day.

There was one tragic irony to each rest stop. Whenever the command was given to resume marching, there would always be those who simply didn't have any further resolve to keep going. Exhausted, frost bitten, hungry, and lacking confidence in a tomorrow, they apparently decided it was useless to prolong the inevitable. While the rest of us moved on, Communist guards would always remain with the fallen survivors. No one had to explain the mission of those lingering guards. We all knew. When we got a comfortable distance from where our fallen comrades were, then came the crackle of distant gunfire. Many of the weary marchers, upon hearing the gunfire, said a mumbled prayer, others made the sign of the cross, still others just kept moving along trance-like, not knowing whether or not the crackle of gunfire after the next rest stop would be for them. Some were even beginning to give the impression of not giving a damn.

We tried to assist as many of the "walking wounded" as best we could. We transported some by way of makeshift sleds. Others were drawn by a horse or mule. Unfortunately, most of those so transported eventually froze to death due to lack of proper garments to keep them warm. My leg and groin injuries had healed sufficiently enough for me to help.

Compounding our troubles was the fact that none of us knew just where, how long or how far we had to travel to reach the encampment. We did know that the farther north we traveled the colder it got. Since, for reasons of security against allied planes, we were forced to travel mostly at night, we had no idea of distance traveled or any indication of approaching villages. We were weary soldiers moving along on weak legs and at the complete mercy and whim of our captors.

One thing, even to this day, that has always angered me is that there never have been any great news accounts documenting the plight of American and allied troops forced to march, primarily at night, 400 miles in sub-zero temperatures on cold, damp grounds through North Korea. While I respect what those brave soldiers endured on Bataan during World War II, I also highly resent the fact that history has all but ignored what we endured during that infamous trek in North Korea. Those troops suffered and suffered badly. Those who died, did so hard.

We finally arrived at the main prison compound in February, 1951. To the man, we were bone weary, half starved and almost dehydrated. But, somehow, we had at least made it to the camp. There was even a fleeting bit of nourishment in the fact that we had cheated death for 400 bloody miles. I don't think any of us really looked ahead to the next day. We just savored that very moment of physical triumph. Dammit! We had walked 400 miles on badly parched corn and a belly full of guts.

There were, I later found out, about six other main prison camps throughout North Korea. We were assigned to Camp 5. Believe me when I say the place was definitely not the New York Hilton. In fact, it didn't even resemble Joe Duncan't Motel back in Arkansas. About forty men were packed into quarters about 12 feet long and 10 feet wide. Each of us had to sleep on one side at a time. Any poor bastard who felt like stretching out was in trouble from the rest of us. Stretching out while sleeping was a luxury

Camp 5 could not afford.

Since none of us had any fat layer between our skin and bones, small scars began to appear on our bodies after a few days. They were caused by the pressure of our tender skin rubbing against the hard floor on which we slept. We would eventually call the scars "pressure sores." After a while, it began to hurt like hell just to lie on the floor. I can remember hearing guys groan at night as they attempted to shift positions and accidentally rubbed the sores against the floor.

Since our captors could care less about our sores, we were forced to come up with some kind of "down home" remedy ourselves. Aggravating the problem was the fact that some of our sores were beginning to stink. I can remember vomiting at least twice because of the stench.

The solution to our problem came from a mild mannered soft spoken POW whom we affectionately called "Poppa Browne." A career soldier, he had seen it all and let very little get next to him. He wasn't more than forty-seven, but he carried himself like a man at least twenty years older. He seldom raised his voice, but when he spoke, the rest of us usually listened. He was a proud black man who placed racial dignity above all else. At first some of us considered Poppa Browne a bit old-fashioned. The brothers in the streets would have called him a hopeless square. He was a total no-nonsense individual. He had a way of talking without ever really looking at you.

"Fellas, got a minute?" Poppa Browne casually asked us one morning as we lounged inside our quarters. He was kneeling near Corporal Jimmy Tucker. Corporal Tucker had lost all of his toes as a result of frostbite during the long journey to camp. Maggots were all over the end of his feet where his toes once were. At least they looked like maggots to me. Since Tucker always kept a heavy towel-like wrapping around his feet, none of us really noticed the maggots before. I know damn well I didn't.

"Fellas," Poppa Browne began rather matter of factly, "the Good Lord placed everything here for a reason." He then bent over and began removing some maggots from Corporal Tucker's feet. "In civilian life," this wily black sergeant continued, "we usually make light of these seemingly worthless little devils." He then took a small handful of maggots and placed them in several small sores on his own right thigh. "But, here in this God-forsaken rat hole," he continued philosophically, "these supposedly worthless little devils become nature's little helpers. They do the Good Lord's will just fine. Y'all see, they're little doctors without degrees."

Poppa Browne, coolly completing placement of the maggots on his sore-riddened thigh, slowly leaned backwards, his stoic disposition evidencing a faint bit of ecstasy as he reclined peacefully on the floor. We all stood stunned as we watched the little maggots nibble aggressively at those sores. "Aw, eat young'ns eat," he signed, his eyes now closed in a bit of rapture.

If this same scene was enacted on any street corner in America, it would be met with howls, hoots, laughter and ridicule. But, on this morning back in 1951, no one dared utter a sound. This was our very first lesson in survival from Poppa Browne. There would be many others.

The subtle brainwashing by our captors began shortly after we arrived at Camp 5. I remember how the Chinese officer that day greeted us tersely:

"Black boys here!"
"White boys there!"
"Filipino boys here!"
"Korean traitors there!"

Each racial grouping filed to the side as the Chinese officer barked his command while pointing in the direction he wanted that grouping to file. That officer was a mean looking little bastard. Nothing polite and humble about him. He looked vicious and out for blood. I had become so accustomed to the Chinese stereotypes in the movies, all the smiling and bowing and so forth. This particular son-of-a-bitch wasn't smiling, not to mention any bowing.

"You there! Move! Move!" the officer yelled at a slow moving white POW. I got the impression that if that white POW had not jumped to it that little midget was prepared to get violent. "You people better obey!; Better obey without trouble!" he bellowed through broken English.

After all the sorting had been done, the Chinese officer adjusted his trousers in a rather pompous manner and headed for us, the black POWs. As he headed in our direction, I remember my reaction quite clearly. "Aw shit!"

It has always amazed me how mild mannered, innocent looking, polite little Chinese civilians become vicious fanatical maniacs during times of war. In fact, as the pompous little screwball headed in our direction, I tried to briefly imagine him as one of those polite little gracious civilians I had seen in San Francisco's Chinatown a few years earlier. Those were gracious and humble people. I used to think the same thing about the Japanese prior to World War II. Bull! These same supposedly humble, mild mannered little midgets were capable of administering the worst kind of physical and psychological torture if they put their minds to it.

"Glad to have you black comrades here," the officer said with a faint smile, almost San Francisco Chinatown style. "I had a very dear black friend when I attended your UCLA several years ago. Any of you guys go to UCLA?"

Stone silence from us. In fact, as I recall, I sort of hoped someone would speak up since the little buzzard was at least trying to be civil. But, no one else spoke up and neither did I. "Anybody from USC?" he continued, still smiling faintly. I really thought for a moment of saying something stupid, like "What about Arkansas AM & N or Grambling?" But, still I, along with the rest, said nothing. No one in his right mind wanted to draw attention to himself, to be singled out. These innocent looking little warriors were dangerous and we all knew it. "No need you guys be 'fraid of us, we your friend. We treat you fair and square." As he continued his patronizing bit of bullshit, I kept my eyes focused on a little fat tobacco chewing guard fingering a mounted machine gun atop a small nearby wagon. He was fingering that thing dangerously, carelessly, while keeping it pointed our way. That guard was a kind of carefree, laid-back sort of guy, one that would simply apologize for accidentally blowing your head off for lack of anything better to do. He looked itchy for action. He reminded me of a gum chewing whore on a busy city street when business was slow and she was broke. When whores get nervous they can pop gum. Well, that clown atop that wagon was nervous too. He wanted something to happen. I got the impression that he really wanted to shoot that goddamn machine gun, preferably at somebody.

I guess I had been staring too intently at the guard atop the wagon because before I knew it he began staring back at me. He slowly swung the machine gun in my direction, letting it come to rest directly on me. That little bastard then winked at me and began to nervously pat the top of the gun, all the time chewing tobacco and spitting over the gun in my direction. I quickly turned my head back toward the Chinese officer, who was now talking about the great black athletes.

"I once saw the great Sugar Ray Robinson," he droned on. "It was in Chicago. He was like Chinese ballet dancer. Good moves. Great fighter. All you should be proud of Sugar Ray. Credit to race. Credit to Third World peoples."

At that particular moment I could care less about Sugar Ray Robinson or Joe Louis. My only concern was a fat tobacco chewing Communist Chinese guard pointing a machine gun at me and occasionally winking. I can't say I felt a slow panic creeping over me. I will say I was concerned, especially when the sucker winked and gave me the finger at the same time.

I again shifted my attention and focus back to the Chinese officer, now beginning to deploy his bag of psychological tricks as he walked slowly in front of us.

"Gentlemen," he began politely, "as long as you have been in the United States Army you blacks have never been recognized as the first in anything. You people always number two or three, but never number one. Here, with us, your Chinese comrades, you now number one. You will be Detachment Number One! Nice, huh?"

Incredible!

That officer had an acute knowledge of U.S. military structure as it existed back in 1951. My thoughts momentarily left Camp 5. I went back to the time I first entered the army back in 1941. It was then that I encountered a Jewish dentist that came to us while I was assigned to the hospital unit. He was very candid, that dentist. He told us that he didn't particularly like us, but that he didn't necessarily hate us either. He explained that as long as we were in the U.S. Army we, as blacks, would always be Detachment Number Two and the white boys Detachment Number One. That meant that if the white boys brought one stick, we were expected to bring two. That little advice was given us in 1941 by an American officer. Now, I was being reminded of it in 1951 by a Communist Chinese officer in North Korea. Incredible!

The Communist Chinese officer then walked over in front of the white POWs. "These people here," the officer yelled while pointing to the white POWs, "they are now Detachment Number Two. You black boys are now Number One. Nice, huh?"

This little five-foot four-inch Chinese officer was taking full advantage of known racial prejudices to plant seeds of possible racial discord in the camp. My thought at the time was that they were wasting absolutely no time getting into the racial bag.

I again turned my attention to the guard on the wagon. The moment my eyes glanced in his direction he once more gave me the finger. Then, as if to dramatically drive home a point of hatred, he climbed down from the wagon, came around on the side, opened his trousers, took out his penis and began urinating, taking care to point himself in my direction. "Damn slob," I remember whispering quietly to myself. "Damn slob!"

# 3
# Two Hours on Ice

Since I was fully aware of the many atrocities perpetrated against the Jews in World War II Nazi concentration camps, I was acutely suspicious of any and all unexplained actions by our captors. I knew full well that our enemy could do anything they wanted to do with us, and probably get away with it if they won the war. What's more, at this particular point in time they were winning the war. As a rule, I am normally not paranoid about many things. However, in 1951, I was quite paranoid about everything.

My paranoia was compounded by the fact that none of our captors seemingly wanted to take any damn responsibility for us. When we first entered the main camp, the Chinese kept telling us we were the sole responsibility of the North Koreans. The Chinese kept saying they were only there to support the North Koreans, not take over from them.

"You no belong to us. We keep tellin' you boys that. You no belong to us. No way."

"You better be nice 'cause we not responsible. We not responsible. North Koreans responsible. You hear me good. They responsible."

Over and over we heard this choppy English monologue from our Chinese captors shortly after we arrived at the main camp. Later, the North Koreans began telling us we were at the complete mercy of the Chinese. The North Koreans said that whatever happened to us would be up to the Chinese. At times, they were quite adamant about it.

"They lie and you know it! They captured you! Why should we own you and they captured you? It's silly! Silly! Chinese responsible for you, not us! Not us!"

Regardless of who owned us, we knew that if we tried to escape, *everyone* would take a shot. There was no debate on this point, at least in our minds.

To fully understand our concern for who "owned" us is to be aware that, for the most part, the North Koreans were a bit intolerant. Keep in mind we had invaded their territory, burned their land, destroyed their crops, shot their friends. Their feelings against us were deep, and we knew it. On the other hand, we had not invaded China, had not destroyed their crops, had not burned their cities. While the Chinese had no great love for us, they could afford to be a bit more tolerant. So, all things being equal, if you had to have your butt beaten on any given day, you sort of wanted it to be administered by the Chinese. The Chinese, in my opinion, did it as if they were doing it for sport. The North Koreans did it more like it was revenge. At any rate, all of this "passing the ownership buck" was very much a cause for concern, at least by me. It was quite similar to a bigoted Southern sheriff turning a black inmate over to a rampaging white mob, saying, in effect, "I won't be responsible." I can imagine that a lot of Nazi concentration camp guards sent Jews to the ovens saying, "I am not responsible." You bet your happy butt they're responsible. What's more, they knew it at the time they did it.

My first confrontation with the conflict over "ownership" came about ten days after we had arrived at Camp 5. I don't recall just what the questions were that had been asked me by two Chinese instructors. In any case I apparently didn't give them satisfactory answers. I was abruptly hauled into the camp commander's office. It appeared that the instructors thought I was having a cottin pickin' "attitude" problem, that I wasn't "cooperating," whatever that was supposed to mean. Looking back, after all these years, maybe I wasn't looking frightened enough to suit them. Maybe they felt the need to install a bit of humility in me.

At any rate, that incident provided my first opportunity to meet "Bop Daddy", the dapper little camp commander. He was about five feet five inches tall and weighed no more than 140-145 pounds. He was a suave little bastard, as smooth as hell. In civilian life he was unquestionably a Chinese Don Juan, a typical lady's man. Cleopatra had her beauty and "Bop Daddy" had his long curly hair. The little buzzard must have combed those curly locks at least once every fifteen minutes. He had this way of talking to you while standing in front of a small mirror styling those curly locks. God! The man was vain. Meticulously dressed at all times, the name "Bop Daddy" was given to him by the black POWs. One other thing about "Bop Daddy", he always spoke to us through an interpreter, although we discovered at the end of our internment that he was quite fluent in English. "Bop Daddy" gave the impression of being a man completely mentally removed from the damn war. He was too laid-back, too nonchalant.

I would bet that this man cared less about Mao Tse-Tung than he did the charms of a lovely woman in his own bedroom. "Bop Daddy" was dangerous in another respect. If, as an example, a guard suggested blowing your damn guts out, "Bop Daddy" would probably run the comb through his hair and say it was just fine with him. The man just didn't give a damn, unless, perhaps, someone spilled blood on his neatly pressed trousers.

"Sit down, comrade," "Bop Daddy" beckoned to me through a Chinese interpreter as I entered his office flanked by the two instructors I supposedly offended.

"Thank you, sir," I recall responding.

"Enjoying it here, comrade?" he continued, rising from his chair and going over to the mirror. "Enjoying our Asian hospitality?"

I started to say something but decided against it for fear of saying something stupid. I had to watch this cagey little bastard. He was too cool, too laid back. I had to read him carefully or it might be my ass. He was now combing his hair and talking to me while looking into the mirror. "Are the Chinese comrades being nice to you, soldier?" he casually asked, never taking his eyes from the mirror as he slowly raked the comb through his hair.

"Er . . . yes . . . yessir," I recall lying. I wondered if he really wanted me to tell him the truth, that they were a bunch of cold-blooded butchers.

"Good. Very good, comrade," he continued. "I was beginning to think my comrades had forgotten the teachings of Chairman Mao. You are familiar with the Chairman, aren't you, comrade?"

"Yessir," I responded nervously, not knowing where in the hell this casual conversation was leading.

After a few moments, a North Korean guard entered the room. He was a big one, with two sidearms hanging from his hips and a large baseball-like bat in his hand.

"This is Comrade Kim-Sing," "Bop Daddy" explained casually. "What do you think of the North Korean guards, comrade?"

"I think they are just fine," I again lied. I really wanted to give a half-hour speech about how much I loved those little Korean monsters. I wanted to kiss the slob if I thought that would prevent "Bop Daddy" from turning me over to them. But "Bop Daddy" apparently cared more for his hair than my black hide, that's for damn sure.

"Bob Daddy" finally managed to get his hair arranged to his satisfaction, then returned to his chair, looking me in the eyes for the first time. He continued his conversation through the Chinese interpreter. "My guards tell me, comrade, that you disobeyed them. Is that true?"

"If I did, sir, it was unintentional. It was not deliberate. I would do nothing to offend any guard in this camp," I lied, quite convincingly I must admit.

"My comrades say you are arrogant and ungrateful. Soldier, are you arrogant and ungrateful . . . or are my comrades lying on you?"

"No . . . No, sir," I continued to lie, "they are not . . . I am not arrogant and ungrateful, at least I don't think I am. I try not to be. I came from a very humble family. I have absolutely no reason, sir, to be arrogant and ungrateful." I tried to keep the answer focused on the arrogant and ungrateful question and to ignore the part dealing with whether or not the guards were lying. That was a Catch-22. Any answer would be damaging to my ass and I knew it.

"Are my comrades lying on you, soldier?"

Shit! I recall thinking, that sucker is sharp. "No, sir," I fumbled, "the guards are not lying." I was trapped and I knew it.

"Soldier, I try my best to remind my comrades of the Geneva Convention, of the teachings of fairness taught by Chairman Mao, but you make it difficult for us. You really do. You force us to discipline you."

Well, here it comes I thought. I braced myself for the worst as "Bop Daddy" left his chair and came over to me, putting one arm around my shoulders.

"Comrade, I am going to give you a break this time," he whispered.

Good, I thought to myself. I really pulled one over this little son-of-a-bitch. This former Arkansas farm boy screwed him around royally, I mused to myself.

"Instead of turning you over to my comrades for punishment," "Bop Daddy" retorted, "I am going to turn you over to Comrade Kim-Sing. After all, the North Koreans actually run this place," he reminded. "We, like you, are only guests here."

I felt sick. I really did. I felt less better when that Kim-Sing idiot began smiling sheepishly while caressing that baseball-like bat. I really felt like begging "Bop Daddy" not to turn me over to the North Koreans. But, I figured that wouldn't do much good. At any rate, "Bop Daddy" was again in front of that mirror and I was being led outside by Comrade Kim-Sing.

I had made up my mind right then and there that if that son-of-a-bitch tried to hit me with that bat I would die trying to defend myself. I was not going to let any man beat me to death like a dog without at least trying to defend myself.

Comrade Kim-Sing hustled me out to a nearby frozen lake and ordered me to take off my shoes. While removing my shoes I kept my eyes trained on that goddamn bat. If he had raised it, I was prepared to die fighting. After I had removed my shoes the beefy Korean ordered me to move out onto the icy lake. I paused for a moment to get myself mentally prepared for this ordeal. I had recognized Kim-Sing as one of the South Korean soldiers assigned to our unit and he could speak English.

"Move!" the bastard shouted, removing his revolver and pointing it at my head.

I moved slowly onto the icy lake. I kept on walking further out, expecting the Korean to fire at my head at any moment.

"Stop!" he finally ordered. "Turn around and face me!"

I obeyed, still not knowing what this bastard was up to.

"Now, you move one foot and you die. You stay still 'till I say move. Understand?"

"Sure," I responded half sarcastically. At first I was determined not to wince, to cry out or to give that little fat ass any type of satisfaction that would come from my agony.

Ten minutes passed and still no outward show of agony from me. Comrade Kim-Sing slowly took out a cigarette, lit it and began inhaling slowly, his revolver now back in his holster.

Twenty minutes passed and by now my wet socks against the icy lake had begun to trigger a burning sensation under my feet. Damn! My feet were beginning to burn, but still I stood without motion. While standing on that ice, I realized that if I were ever going to truly call myself a man in later life, I had to somehow survive this little ordeal without giving in to what I really felt like doing, screaming like all hell. But, I didn't scream. I vowed not to let Comrade Kim-Sing break my spirit. Again, I wasn't being courageous, just plain stubborn.

Somewhere I once read that Socrates or Aristotle, or one of those brilliant Greeks, had stood barefooted in sub-zero temperatures and survived without even a slight head cold. According to the story, that Greek used his vivid imagination to mentally thrust himself into one of the most humid parts of Africa on one of the hottest days ever. As the story goes, when the temperatures where the Greek was standing began to drop even further he actually began to sweat profusely as he continued to imagine the hot sun beating down on him in deepest Africa. Well, for lack of a better alternative I decided to test the validity of that old Greek story. I closed my eyes and began to force myself to concentrate, driving my mind back to my early years in Arkansas, back into the hot fields on a blistering July afternoon. It had always been a bitch in Arkansas in July and August. I thought about how my parents would admonish us to work harder in the fields because we really needed the money. I used to marvel at how my parents worked in that blistering sun without ever complaining or even seemingly being aware that the sun was bearing down. They were true stoics, something I was trying to be on that icy lake in North Korea back there in 1951. Either some historians lied on those Greeks or their imaginations were a hell of a lot more powerful than mine. My feet still felt the biting pain caused by the icy floor against my socks. Forty-five minutes passed and still I stood without wincing on that lake. I never took my eyes off that Comrade Kim-Sing. Then, a break! I noticed that he was beginning to shiver a bit. The cold was actually getting to the bastard, and he wasn't even out there on the ice! I had a chance to break his spirits! If only my now numb feet would hold out. The feeling was nearly gone.

"Hey, Comrade Kim-Sing, sir!" I managed to yell out as casual as I could.

"Yeah!" he responded, his voice quivering from the cold. I decided to really mess with his mind and at the same time save me.

"Ever been to Arkansas?" I asked matter of factly.

"Dunno," he responded, making absolutely no sense whatsoever. He then took out another cigarette and could hardly hold the thing between his trembling fingers. The buzzard was cold as hell, and I was nearly frozen, but I was beginning to enjoy the damn ordeal.

"After you guys win the war," I continued, stepping up my attack, "You should map out you a plot of land in Arkansas. Good soil, Good place to grow some rice and soy beans. Take my word for it, you'd be rich in no time."

"Don't wanna be rich," he snorted.

The bastard was cold and I knew it.

Instead of continuing the small talk I decided to do the impossible. I started whistling "Dixie." Imagine a black man whistling "Dixie" anywhere at anytime. But, here I was, whistling "Dixie" on an icy lake in North Korea. I must say I whistled the hell out of that rebel song. I could see a seething anger coming over Comrade Kim-Sing.

"Quiet!" he blurted. "Quiet or I keep you here all night. Freeze you to death!" He and I both knew he'd have to remain out there with me. I was getting to him. The bastard was breaking. By now I was nearly insane with pain, but I was determined to stick it to him. I guess Comrade decided to make one last ditch effort to break my spirits. Just shooting me would be a moral victory for me and I knew Comrade Kim-Sing knew it. He walked out on the ice, about four feet from me, took out his penis and began urinating directly in front of me. For people who had little going for them they sure as hell didn't mind showing it off. Finishing his business, he shook himself gingerly, then replace his penis and left the ice. I thought about that for a moment, then decided to make the supreme act of defiance. I slowly took out my own penis and began urinating on the ice.

"Don't piss on the ice!" he shouted. "Don't you piss on the ice! I shoot you if you piss on the ice!" He quickly removed his revolver and I quickly replaced my penis.

"Sorry, Comrade, sir, sorry."

I felt absolutely nothing in my feet. I expected to fall at anytime. But, I kept a smile on my face and continued to look at Comrade. I wondered what it was about war that made two total strangers want to blow the other's guts out. Comrade Kim-Sing was perhaps a damn good family man. He no doubt went to his Buddhist temple regularly and walked in the parks with his wife and children. However, war had changed him into such a monster until he was prepared to blow my brains out for urinating on a worthless icy lake. The irony of it all is that I, too, was a family man who visited church every Sunday and was very much in love with my family. I respected other people and usually went out of my way to help. I almost had a serious auto accident once trying to avoid hitting a dog. But, on this day in January 1951, I was fully prepared, if given the opportunity, to cut Kim-Sing's goddamn throat and not think a thing about it. I was no better than he. He just happened to have the gun. We were both brutal animals of the worst sort and I knew it. At that particular moment love of country and all that bull had nothing to do with it. I wanted to kill this son-of-a-bitch before he had a chance to kill me. It was just as simple as that.

"Wanna go back now, boy?" Kim-Sing asked rather sarcastically.

"It's up to you, Comrade," I lied, trying my best to sound indifferent and casual. "I'm sorta gettin' used to being out here. Kinda gives me a chance to meditate, to sort things out, know what I mean?"

"Why do whites call you boys niggers?"

"Well, 'cause they're ignorant and don't know any better," I retaliated. "They're really cowards when you come right down to it. Anybody who calls us niggers is a no-good God-forsaken dirty coward." I remember saying this with no attempt whatsoever to conceal my bitterness. I was now quite tired and totally numb in the feet. In fact, I had to spread my arms a bit to retain my balance. It was getting a bit serious out there and I was getting a bit "I don't give a dammish."

Kim-Sing was from South Korea and had apparently been around white troops who indoctrinated him in the treatment of blacks.

"I agree with the whites," Kim-Sing blurted back, obviously too. He then took out his revolver and aimed it at my feet. "Am I too ignorant soldier?"

"You couldn't be Comrade," I lied quickly, "you ain't quite white."

"Next time you wise off, nigger, we bring you back out here and bury your black ass under white ice. You smart nigger! You smart! We have ways to deal with smart niggers. You see! You see!"

I was already seeing and feeling, but I was determined not to break. In all fairness, I really didn't know how much longer I would be able to remain on my numb feet. Since Kim-Sing was still shivering. I thought if I only didn't fall he would give up and call off the ordeal.

If I fell, however, I knew he would be encouraged to stay longer, perhaps all night, to delight in my ordeal. I just had to take the fight out of this bastard. As a race, we had survived slavery. I just had to survive this sucker. I decided to gamble. I started humming the melody to one of Duke Ellington's favorites, "Satin Doll." I remember pretending to really be carried away by what I was doing. I even began to snap my fingers and twist my butt to the beat of my humming. I got louder and louder and pretended to be more carried away. One thing I learned about the Koreans and the Chinese, if they thought you were crazy, they didn't bother to waste too much time with you. They only messed with you if they considered you intelligent. I had to stop acting like I was intelligent. I had to become insane. So, me and Duke's "Satin Doll" went to it.

"I said no sing!" Kim-Sing shouted. "No sing!"

Now came the moment of truth. I had to make my move. If I stopped he owned me. If I continued, I could also be shot. But, if my gamble paid off, I might have an advantage, small as it may be. I opted to keep singing, only louder.

"Aw, shucks! Do it to me, mama, do it to me now!" I shouted between my melodious humming.

"Goddammit! No sing!" Kim-Sing again shouted, now taking out his revolver and pointing at my feet.

I kept up the humming, now intensifying my butt shaking and finger snapping. Either it worked or I would die on an icy lake while shaking my ass to the tune of Duke's immortal "Satin Doll."

Kim-Sing fired two shots near my feet. "No sing nigger! Can't you hear? I say no sing. No sing!" Again he fired near my feet.

I began to again snap my fingers and move my butt to the rhythm of my humming. I was very careful to keep the grin broad.

It was now a standoff. He looked at me as if to say I don't believe this black idiot.

Kim-Sing then moved slowly around me in a circle. I really couldn't tell whether he was seeking a better position from which to swing that bat . . . or to discern what the hell was happening to me mentally. I stood motionless but kept up the humming, quite loudly I should add. He continued to circle slowly, very much like a prize fighter jockeying for an opening in his opponent's defenses. I must admit that he was beginning to play hell with my own psyche. I was becoming more than uneasy. Still, I kept humming loudly, trying all the time to keep him in sight through the corner of my eyes. I didn't dare turn my head. I figured that if I turned my head to follow his motions, he would see straight through my little insane routine. I had to be very convincing in my seemingly "out of it state." Kim-Sing had to believe that I was in my own little world, that I didn't know he was even there. I also had to caution myself not to get so hung up doing my routine that I forgot that a little son-of-a-bitch was circling me with a damn bat bent on smashing my brains. I had to keep up my routine without forgetting my focus. Then it happened. He shouted and at the same time slammed the bat into the ground directly behind me. I almost died! I was so sure that little sucker had hit me. But, I never lost my composure. I kept humming and snapping my fingers to the beat. I decided to stop moving my butt. I was trying to do too much physically while trying to keep my mind on him mentally.

He again shouted and slammed the bat into the ground behind me, a bit closer this time. It didn't have quite the same mental impact this time because I was more or less anticipating some kind of action.

He kept up the circling. I kept up the humming, and the finger snapping. I don't know how much I was getting to him mentally, but he was sure as hell getting all of my attention with that bat and those circling movements, especially those behind me. The fact that he never said anything was really playing havoc with my attempts to keep up the routine I was doing. That bastard was psyching the hell out of me. At one point I almost forgot the melody to "Satin Doll."

"Nigger!" Kim-Sing finally called out, breaking the silence. "Betcha I can smash skull with one blow. One blow. Wanna bet nigger boy? Wanna bet?"

He now began to dance around me, swinging the bat back and forth in front of him as he danced. I became louder with my humming.

"Nigger!" he again called out. "One blow! Whatcha bet, huh, nigger, watcha bet?" When he danced behind me with that bat, I tried to strain my eyes as far as possible in an effort to determine whether or not the bastard was about to strike. He was cute alright.

"Nigger! Whatcha bet, huh? Whatcha bet? Don't wanna bust head without a bet nigger. Must have bet. Hear me nigger?

Whatcha bet I can bust head in one blow. Smash like watermelon. Like watermelon, nigger?"

From the distance I managed to hear someone calling out in either Korean or Chinese, couldn't really make out which. I slowly brought my humming to a halt when I realized the voice in the distance was calling Kim-Sing.

He turned and responded in Korean and the two talked for about a minute before Kim-Sing turned his attention again to me. "Time to go," he snapped. "No smash your watermelon today. Maybe later, huh, nigger. Maybe later?"

"Up your ass," I recall whispering to myself as we headed from the lake. Again, at least temporarily, I had cheated death or serious injury.

I was brought back to the main compound and again turned over to the Chinese. They, in turn, placed me in a dimly lit damp basement. After being on that icy lake for two hours, the basement, cold as it was, still felt warm. I huddled in a corner, removed my wet socks and began massaging my feet. They were still numb. I tried as best I could to survey my surroundings. I could hear the sound of water dripping but I was too tired to investigate where it was. I did make out what appeared to be several large seemingly unusable machines of some type. Since webs were all over the items I managed to see, I concluded that the basement was not used very much. One thing for sure, it was not suitable for human habitation. From time to time I could see large rats darting back and forth. God! How I've always hated rats! I spent several days in Harlem once and the thing I remember most about that place was not the Apollo, which I enjoyed, but the rats!

Although I was cold and exhausted, I knew damn well I wasn't going to fall asleep with those little creatures roaming around out there. Looking back, it seems silly to have worried about rats when upstairs men had guns. But, I was still concerned about those rats. They represented an immediate danger. I knew full well that hungry men ate rats out of desperation. I also knew that rats were capable of doing the same to men, especially one stupid enough to fall asleep in a cold damp basement in North Korea.

It's funny, really, the phenomena that take place within one's mind and body amid a climate of fear. Prior to seeing the rats I was suffering miserably from the damp coldness. After I sighted the little bastards, I actually became warm. Coldness was no longer a chief concern. The rats solved that little problem.

After a while I could no longer see the rats but I could hear them. I kept my feet tucked up under me as I sat on the floor huddled in a corner. Every now and then I would stomp hard on the floor in an effort to chase the rats further from me. At one point I stood up and ran in place, as tired as I was. They say noise usually conquers fear in many situations. I reasoned that the rats would be frightened like all hell hearing my feet pound against the floor and seeing this lanky old black going up and down. It apparently worked because they disappeared. I again sat huddled on the floor, my thoughts again turning to how damn cold it was now becoming.

I guess about three hours passed before a light flicked on in a basement room adjoining mine. I heard what appeared to be at least three men beating up someone they had just dragged into the room. I quickly crawled over to the wall dividing that room from mine, already concluding that it was no doubt an American POW who was getting it, although I heard no English. At first I couldn't find a crack in the wall large enough for me to see through. Quite frankly I didn't need to see what I heard to be fists and feet slamming into the man being beaten. He was screaming out in either Korean or Japanese, I could not immediately tell which. I was at least relieved that it was not an American, especially not this one. I kept searching for a crack in the wall while the beating continued. I finally climbed up on one of the old machines where I could peek through an opening near the ceiling. By now the beating had stopped. I thought the victim was by now either dead or unconscious. When I peeked in I discovered that the man, a Korean or Japanese soldier, was being dragged over to a small wash tub. He was a bloody mess. The three guards, all Chinese, took a water hose, hooked it up, turned it on, and began forcing the nozzle down the screaming boy's throat. God! Believe me when I say they were wasting no time being gentle. That kid struggled for life and death. I almost threw up watching that scene. Finally, the soldier stopped struggling, his body falling limply to the floor. The three Chinese soldiers said something, laughed, then removed and washed the now bloody hose and left the room. I froze my position, not seeking to draw attention to my own presence next door. I didn't know what the hell was going on and I sure as hell wasn't going to ask questions.

They only kept me overnight in the basement before returning me to my quarters. Most of the guys were shocked but delighted when I stumbled back into the quarters.

I made my way over to Poppa Browne and was about to explain my ordeal to him when he interrupted.

"I ain't interested in what ya been through, Thompson, only that ya managed to survive. We still have to make it through tomorrow. So don't waste yo' time braggin' 'bout today."

When he said this, he never once looked me directly in the eye. There was no anger, no bitterness, only a lot of common sense.

# 4
# Propaganda Victims

For a black Arkansas farm boy, fresh meat is a staple for every meal. Doesn't matter whether it's red beans and rice or collard greens and okra, there is always meat. As a race, black people eat a lot. Since most blacks are born into poverty, they have always managed to find solace in good soul food and good Baptist preaching. We can take the preaching much better after a good meal . . . or in anticipation of a good one. Many Baptist churches in the black community serve large "pot luck" meals after the sermons. A "pot luck" is delightful because of the potential to get a variety of good food.

All the Church members pitch in and bring something.

You name it and it's brought: chitterlings, roast pork, potato salad, black eyed peas and red beans, collard and mustard greens, ham hocks and pig tails, fried and smothered chicken, turkey, string beans, gumbo, corn bread, an assortment of pies. To say it again, black folk, despite their poverty, have always managed to eat well. Maybe not the best of food, but a lot of the worst.

So, it was more than a cultural shock for us to be fed chiefly boiled and parched corn, a little fish and a little rice. Since the latter two were traditional Chinese and Korean delicacies, you bet we weren't given much of those. Meat was out of the question! They also gave us some kind of boiled seeds that even today I don't know what they were or if they really had any nutritional values.

Another thing about our diet in camp, there was no salt. Here again, this struck hard at blacks who traditionally eat a lot of salt. The average black, especially those born in the South, usually sprinkles a quantity of salt on a meal even before it is sampled. This is usually followed by an ample portion of hot sauce. It is small wonder then that one out of every four blacks is believed to be a victim of high blood pressure. We, as a race, love a lot of salt and highly seasoned food. Take away these items and food, to us, is too bland and not worthy of being eaten until we are half starved most of the time.

The Koreans and Chinese knew a great deal about our dietary habits and put this knowledge to great use in propaganda campaigns. I remember a time I was sent to pick up some rations and was grabbed by two Korean guards. They hustled me off to a corner, gave me a large slab of meat, and told me to smile and hold it up. They wanted to take pictures of me holding it. They snapped pictures of me with that meat for almost fifteen minutes, using all type angles. I swear I could have eaten that slab raw. I felt good just holding that meat. After the photo session, they took back the slab and told me to get on with whatever it was I was supposed to be doing.

At other times, in other photo sessions, they would march groups of us up into the hills, order us to remove our shoes and clothing and stack them neatly on the ground. They would then order us to step back while they took pictures of the shoes and clothing. Then they took additional pictures of them issuing the clothes to us. This, I suppose, was to publicly document their splendid treatment of POWs.

Back to food. We were told by our captors that 800 grams of

food a day was enough for us to survive on and that is exactly what they gave us. The body is a marvelous machine. I soon discovered that when you are accustomed to getting only small quantities of food, it only takes a little to satisfy. When you are accustomed to a large amount, you crave that large amount even when you don't need it. In camp, however, there were serious questions as to whether or not we were getting enough of the minimum on which to survive.

It wasn't too long before the dying began. We would bed down at night only to arise from time to time to discover that someone had died of starvation. Death, as bad as it was, provided some advantage to the survivors. When someone died, we simply did not report that death immediately. Instead, we just put in for that person's rations and divided them among the rest of us. Some may call this unthinkable. We considered it still another vehicle for survival. When we said grace, however, we took care to acknowledge from whom the extra rations came. We were thankful for every additional crumb. Every crumb. We managed to hide the death of one companion for three days. We just could not keep it hidden any longer. We found this easier to do in the winter. When summer came the stench forced us to commit almost immediately.

Propaganda was not only used to convince the outside world that we were being treated humanely by the Chinese and Korean Communists, it was used to great effect in fermenting racial discord among the POWs.

I remember quite vividly how we were all ordered to assemble for "Bop Daddy" one morning. Although the white and black POWs were quartered separately, we did share certain mutual duty responsibilities. No one knew just what to expect. We stood in formation for about a half hour before "Bop Daddy" made his royal and grand entrance. The black POWs were in one formation and the whites in another. The Turks, Japanese/Koreans and other allied POWs were so grouped according to nationality. However, "Bop Daddy" had made sure the white and black

# True Colors

POWs were lined up across from each other.

"Bop Daddy," flawlessly dressed as always, walked down the space separating the black POWs from the whites and began to speak through his interpreter.

"Will Sergeant Nelson Riley please step forward," the interpreter began for "Bop Daddy."

At that point, a stockily built white POW, a new arrival, stepped forward slowly. With red hair and freckles, he looked like a typical practical joker, the type that always shows up in any man's army. He had a somewhat sheepish grin on his face, the type that says "I don't take all of this seriously at all!"

Sergeant Riley began to squirm a bit; he really looked more embarrassed than frightened.

"Sergeant Riley told us he not accustomed to living and eating with you black boys. He tell us this not way he raised. Sergeant Riley say you blacks inferior. Yet . . . you blacks still willin' to fight and even die for people like Sergeant Riley. I no understand you black comrades. Why you willin' to do this? Why? We Chinese your friend. You fight us. Sergeant Riley your enemy. You die for him. You black boys confused. You all mixed up. We try to help you. We defend you 'gainst the Sergeant Rileys while here. You see. We your friends."

Sergeant Riley looked a bit nervous for the first time. He glanced briefly in our direction, then let his eyes fall once again to the ground.

"One thing we want impress on you this morning," "Bop Daddy" continued through his choppy speaking interpreter, "we Chinese see all men as equal. No difference. Absolutely no difference."

Whatever "Bop Daddy" was leading up to we knew to be wary of it. "This white soldier here . . . this, er . . . Sergeant Riley," "Bop Daddy" groped, "now he just joined us yesterday. Just yesterday!"

Sergeant Riley looked sheepishly at the ground, very much akin to a man caught in the bedroom with his neighbor's wife. He has no logical defense.

"Sergeant Riley no believe as we do. He from Laurel, Mississippi. He example of true imperialist. His kind reason we fight war. His kind reason we all here."

"Bop Daddy," as nonchalant as ever, brushed his God-given curly locks, adjusted his trousers, then walked slowly in front of the black formation. He surveyed us for a few minutes, then continued in a rather fatherly tone while looking directly at us.

"I don't want you black boys to be 'fraid of whites anymore. Chairman Mao tell us that a man inferior only in his own mind. A man can enslave himself. He need no help from others. You blacks must stop enslaving yourselves. You must stand up to whites. Make 'em kneel 'fore you sometime."

This cunning little pompous bastard knew the sensitive spots all right. He had done his goddamn homework.

"Bop Daddy" walked casually back over to Sergeant Riley. "Kneel Riley!" he shouted to the American through the interpreter. Riley sank slowly to the ground in front of "Bop Daddy." There was obvious defiance in the way he sank to the ground.

"Stand up Riley!" "Bop Daddy" shouted.

Riley arose slowly, again displaying an obvious defiance.

Regardless of the man's politics, you had to admire his courage.

"Riley, you drop to ground in hurry when I say. You drop in hurry! You try again. Okay? Try again in hurry when I say."

He stood back from Riley about two feet.

"Riley kneel!"

Again Riley stubbornly obeyed, sinking to the ground slower than before.

"Bop Daddy" became enraged. He let go with a vicious karate kick to Riley's face, knocking him backwards. "Bop Daddy" then shouted a command in Chinese and two guards rushed over and picked Riley up, his face now a bloody mess. Once the guards had him standing erect again. "Bop Daddy" stepped forward.

"Riley kneel!"

This time Riley didn't even bother to kneel. He just stood erect—his bloody face staring ahead blankly.

Again "Bop Daddy" unleashed a karate kick, this time to Riley's groin, doubling him over as he tumbled quickly to the ground, his hands cupping his groin; Riley emitted a soft groan, but there were no shouts, no screams, just total defiance in agony.

Once more the guards rushed over and quickly stood a weakened Riley erect.

"Riley kneel! Damn you kneel!" "Bob Daddy" again commanded.

Again Riley stood, his now weakened body swaying a bit, blood from his face now dripping on his trousers. My eyes began to moisten as I stood watching one of the greatest displays of personal courage I had ever witnessed. This kind of stuff happened only in the movies. But, this was not the movies and Camp 5 was not a theater. This was for real and a man was risking his life in order to retain his dignity.

"Bop Daddy" once more cut loose with a karate-like kick, this time to the stomach, again doubling Riley as he slumped to the ground writhing in an agony we all somehow felt.

"Why doesn't the big moron kneel?" someone in my formation asked rhetorically. "Why doesn't the big lug kneel? What's he trying to prove?"

The two guards rushed over to again pick Riley up but he waved them away, opting to try to get up by himself. He tried at least three times to pull himself up, falling back to the ground at each attempt.

"Stay down you bastard! Stay down goddammit!" a voice from the white formation rang out.

Riley, stubborn as ever, ignored the warning, managed to struggle once more to his feet, barely able to control his balance. I had been through some of the most vicious of circumstances during World War Two, but I had never witnessed a circumstance where a man put his raw personal courage against almost certain death . . . all for the sake of dignity. God, I admired that! Someone once said it is better to die with dignity rather than live without it. Apparently, Sergeant Riley had made his decision.

"Riley kneel! Now!" "Bop Daddy" pressed.

Riley again stoically ignored the order, closing his eyes as if in anticipation of the next blow. "Bop Daddy" wasted little time resuming his attack. He sliced Riley across the left side of his neck with a tremendous right hand karate chop. Riley slammed to the ground, lying motionless for about two minutes while the rest of us held our breaths.

"Bop Daddy" moved around Riley slowly, as if trying to decide whether to kick the fallen victim or to keep up his attempts to get him to kneel.

Riley's huge frame began to stir slowly. He tried repeatedly to get to his feet, again tumbling backwards at every attempt.

"Stay down you big lovely son-of-a-bitch! Stay down!" came the cry from Poppa Browne in a rare show of emotion from him.

Again Riley tumbled backwards as he attempted to rise.

"Stay down Riley!" came a similar cry from the formation of blacks.

"Stay down Riley!" another from the formation of whites.

Then, almost like a beautifully trained chorus the entire assemblage took up the chants in unison.

"Stay down Riley! Stay down Riley! Stay down Riley! Stay down Riley! Stay down Riley!"

Riley paused in his attempts, looked around at this massive show of American comaraderie and tumbled backwards to the ground. Immediately a chorus of cheers rang out. I will never fully understand my feelings that day, but if someone were to have asked me to take Riley's place, I probably would have. Such was the passion of the moment.

Weeks later, all of us smuggled notes to Riley, praising his courage and discrediting the racial allegations made by the Communists. About two months after that incident Riley was transferred to another camp. He had apparently become too much of a local hero at Camp 5.

As for the racial allegations, we, the blacks, knew full well how accomplished the Chinese were in distorting the results of any interrogation. If the Chinese asked, for example, whether or not you ever lived with, say, blacks, and you said 'no', this was later interpreted as "his family didn't raise him to live with blacks."

The Chinese were artisans at blending fact and fiction to their own advantage. However, one thing they kept misreading was the American spirit. Given all the ills America has, we, as a people become one family when put upon by an outside common foe. I don't think the Germans or the Japanese understood this during World War Two. I know damn well the Chinese and Koreans didn't during the Korean conflict. Sergeant Nelson Riley was only a symbol of an American's resolve to win . . . to be free. This is the same resolve that saw America through two world wars. This is the same resolve that had sustained black Americans since the days of slavery.

The propaganda war was intensified by the Communists about three weeks into our imprisonment. This, too, was waged along racial lines with blacks used as pawns.

The Communist would take, say, four blacks into an interrogation room, making sure the white POWs saw them go into the room. Several hours after they had been seen entering the room, two guards wearing aprons and carrying cooking utensils and food, including meat fully displayed, followed them into the interrogation room. Again, all of this show was done in full view of the white POWs. The idea was to plant suspicion in the minds of the white POWs that we, the blacks, were collaborating and were being rewarded accordingly. To heighten the suspicion, the Communists would take the interrogated blacks off the heavy work detail and reassign them to something lighter, more desirable.

I didn't realize the extent of what was going on until I was taken into the interrogation room along with two other blacks. Upon entering we were offered American cigarettes, which we all refused. Our refusal came not from any particular act of defiance, but because we simply didn't smoke. I might add that later in the spring of 1951, when we were issued tobacco and a cup of raw sugar, blacks would trade their tobacco to the whites for their sugar. Through this arrangement, I acquired a life long white friend, Bill Lillis.

Bill was as close to a brother as I had ever known, with the exception of Hank, my hometown buddy from Arkansas. Bill was a super guy, highly intelligent. He was sent to the hard labor camp. I remember the morning when he passed by me as he was being marched away in a three column formation. Damn it, they knew our formation! He told me, "Be careful, they are after you."

Finally, Bill returned and we hooked up again. We would walk every day in the courtyard. Once he said, "Jim, what if we returned and the Army was integrated? Hell! Don't worry," I said. "We will be dead long before that." Then Bill pulled out the Chinese Daily News from his pocket. It stated General Ridgeway said we could not fight a dark race and remain segregated.

I looked at Bill. My mind flashed back to the time when "Bop Daddy" made a statement that black soldiers were proud people but should do more reading. Dammit!, this was all coming home. My friend Bill had been reading and I had not. I began to realize that integration was finally becoming a fact in the Armed Forces. No matter that President Truman had issued an Executive Order integrating the Armed Service in 1948, four years earlier.

I felt like an idiot. Both the captors, and my good friend were saying, "Damn it, READ!" To me, Bill set the example of what our constitution means.

As I write this, I blow TAPS to a great American, Bill Lillis. What a pity color of skin had kept us apart so long.

God Bless You, Bill.

"Tobacco and Sugar", what a powerful ambassador.

We were then given a briefing on the war effort, how well things were going for the Communists and how bad things were for the Americans and our allies. Since we were captured in the midst of a major retreat, what we were told could not be totally ignored although the truth was highly suspect. We were then told that a special place had been reserved for POWs who cooperated and aided the Communists in their war effort.

About fifteen minutes after we had entered the room, the two apron wearing guards entered, staggering from the weight of food and cookery. They immediately set up a portable burner and commenced cooking, grandly tossing meat in the skillet first. The idea was to fill the room with the smell of cooking meat. To a half starved man surviving off a diet of boiled and parched corn with minimum rice and fish, the smell of cooking meat was pure torture. The idea apparently was to weaken our resolve so that we would become willing prisoners, ready to make any accommodation for a bit of meat. Unfortunately, the smell and the popping of the meat in the hot pot only served to destroy our concentration. To make things more difficult, the meat being cooked smelled like fresh pork. In fact, I would lay odds it was pig. We had butchered enough of them in Arkansas during my childhood. I know damn well when pork of any kind is being cooked. These little sons-of-bitches were boiling fresh pork! When the little fat guard began to pour seasoning on the meat he also began to hum a little tune. The other guard busied himself preparing the rice and something that resembled celery, but I don't think it was celery. Mind you, this was all being done while the two interrogators kept up their attack on our resolve.

"Tink about it comrades, we already made you Detachment One and white boys Detachment Two. We show we your good friend, right?"

I noticed that the little fat guard dropped a piece of pork on the floor. It was a very small piece. He picked it up, raised the window and threw it out. The other two black POWs also witnessed the meat tossing. I would lay odds we all made a mental note where that window was located. If possible, we would attempt to find that piece of pork later that night.

"Let's put it 'nother way, fellas," one of the interrogators droned on, "they treat you like dogs in States and we try treat you like men here . . . and this prison. Why make life harder for you? Must learn to take it easy when can. We can be nice . . . very nice to you. Quicker you help, quicker we end bad war. You then go home to family and live better with our help. Okay fellas?"

The little fat guard got a long fork and lifted a piece of pork up to survey it. God! That damn meat looked good! I have always been told that pork was bad for me. That it was a leading contributor to high blood pressure among blacks. I was forever told to "stay away from that grease, cut down on that salt, give up all pork even though y'all like it jest fine." I was certainly aware of the logic in these warnings. Under most normal circumstances I am the type to heed most of them. But, this was not a normal circumstance. My mind and body begged for just one bite of that pork, wishing it had been fried with plenty of salt, but here salt was a hard to come by item, as the Chinese didn't use it. I have always considered the smell of cooked bacon early in the morning one of the most delightful of treats. In fact, we used to have a saying, "no matter how difficult things were for a black man, if he could look forward to a plate of red beans and rice with three large ham hocks or pig feet, he could withstand most agonies thrust upon him." I do believe this. To understand this, one has to be black and one has to have lived a black experience. A lot of food and a lot of religion somehow found their way into the black household even during the days of slavery."

"Some day Third World people rule world," the interrogator continued. "You blacks are members of Third World race. You obligated to help win war 'gainst oppressive imperialists. You stupid to fight for aggressors who look down on you. You help us. We look at you like blood brothers. We your kin."

The second guard began to cut up some garlic and spread bean sauce on the pork. He then added water to the pot. He was, I thought, making gravy! They were cooking smothered pork with gravy and rice! These sons-of-bitches were cooking smothered pork with rice and gravy! So it appeared.

"Tell us, would you say morale of you troops low or high? Before you captured, I mean?"

"My name is Sergeant Harley Mims," one of the other black POWs chimed in quickly, "my serial number is . . ." "Shut up!" the interrogator interrupted, slapping him lightly across the face. "We don't want you make us abuse you. Don't doubt our intelligence. Don't play games or you be hurt. You be hurt badly. We your friends. You behave like we are all friends, okay?"

One of the guards who was cooking came to the table with plates, placing one in front of each of us and the others in front of the two interrogators. He then stacked hefty portions of pork, rice and broth gravy on the plates in front of the interrogators but nothing on ours. Both interrogators paused from their questioning and began digging into their meal. The lead interrogator stuffed his goddamn mouth so full until rice and broth slid down the side of his mouth.

At one point he took a piece of pork in both hands, belched, then sank his cotton pickin' teeth into the meat. As he slowly chewed each greasy mouthful, he stared blankly at each of us. But, neither he nor the other interrogator said anything for the first few minutes. The second interrogator was at least eating civilly. The other bastard was a pig eating a pig. I can truly say I hated that son-of-a-bitch! I wanted to slam that pork down his damn throat! I knew, however, that if I managed to get my hands on a piece, his throat would be a secondary consideration to my own mouth. The lead interrogator beckoned for the cooks to bring more food to the table. I think all three of us at that moment searched our souls for what we might wish to give up for a piece of pork. One thing for sure, we would not do or say anything that might prove helpful to the enemy or harmful to us as civilians later on, as this was still 1951 and racism in the States was still on the rampage. We didn't have to be warned that any court martial for us would be deadly. Our courage was borne more out of common sense than anything else. We knew damn well these people didn't love us anymore than they did our white counterparts.

As it turned out, we didn't even have to make a decision regarding what we would give up for a piece of pork. When the guards returned to the table with the food, he poured the remainder on the plates of the two interrogators.

"You black boys like smuthered pork, don'tcha?" the lead interrogator asked, again stuffing his filthy mouth with that pork.

"It's SMOTHERED pork, sir," Sergeant Mims volunteered.

"Thank you for correcting me, comrade," the lead interrogator quipped.

"Beggin' yo' pardon, suh," Sergeant Dale Evans, the other black POW asked, "but kin I have some of dat poke?"

"Was the morale of your troops low or high, Sergeant?" the second interrogator asked. "Just tell us that and we'll discuss what's on my plate. I'm good 'n' full anyway. Was morale good or bad?"

"I jes wants me a small portion, suh, that's all. Just a small portion to quench me appetite," Evans begged. Initially, my reaction was one of hostility toward him for resorting to begging. After a moment, however, I realized he only had the guts to perhaps say aloud what Mims and I were secretly longing to do.

The lead interrogator sensed the softening among us and emptied the remains on his plate onto the plate of the second interrogator.

"Answer him comrade and you eat all this. Share nothing with friends. You reasonable man, comrade. You wise. Answer question. Then eat."

"Can't rightly do that now suh, I'se a soldier. I'se 'pose to give y'all only me name and serial number and nuttin' else. Nuttin' else. Now kin I have yo' plate now suh?"

"But, comrade, you no answer our question. You know we no give 'til you do. That's fair. That's fair. Don't you know that's only fair?" The lead interrogator was now speaking in a most patronizing and condescending manner, fully aware now that Sergeant Evans was not an educated man.

"Naw suh, I know it ain't fair. But it ain't right neither for me to give y'all mo'n me name and me serial number. Not long's I'se a soldier. I can't do dat, suh."

"Sure you can, comrade. Sure you can. Just trust us. It be all right. You good man, comrade. You good man."

"Naw suh," Evans responded sheepishly, "I jes dunno 'bout dat. I don't suh."

The two interrogators glanced at each other briefly, apparently concluding that this ignorant black POW simply wasn't going to cave in to their demands.

"Jest a small piece, suh?" Evans again begged. "De lil' piece on dat side of yo' plate?" Evans pointed to the right side of the interrogator's plate, his finger coming quite close to the food.

"No! No, comrade, please don't touch the food until I give permission. That's no-no. Tell you what, comrade, I understand your loyalty. I really do. Tell me, before capture, were you happy with your comrades?"

"Yes suh. I'se pretty happy."

"That's good, comrade. Very good."

The bastards! I just knew they were about to level their big psychological guns at Evans, to take full advantage of his obvious ignorance.

"Comrade," the lead interrogator began calmly," in a few months this war be over. You all then go home. Important for your family, your little children, that you come back home. Ten years from now you be at park, at beaches with your family. People forget what happen here. Make little sense risk starvation, risk dying here over a little innocent information we want. You agree, comrade? You agree?"

"Naw, naw suh, I don't. I'se black. I do wrong over here and I suffer the rest of me life back home. I dunno, suh."

Sensing a golden opportunity the lead interrogator pounced on Evans' last response.

"That's just the point, comrade. You blacks in United States treated like dogs. Why protect people who don't treat you like we do, like men? Comrade we talk to you like equal . . . not like you inferior to us. Right?"

"I suppose, suh."

"Then reject imperialist way. Cooperate with us and we make life better for you here, guarantee good future for family at home. Trust us, comrade. We your friend."

The second interrogator picked up a piece of pork and raised it slowly to his damn mouth, careful to tantalize the hell out of us. To be true, we all followed the trajectory of that pork until it sank into that son-of-a-bitch's little mouth. Once he had placed it in his mouth, he then rolled it around a bit, pretending to savor every bite. As he chewed, he glanced at us with a sort of "screw you" look.

I wanted to ram my big black foot squarely down that little sucker's mouth. I had to do something. The defiance inside me was now uncontrollable rage. I had to strike back, as insane as it was. I raised my hand as if to scratch my head but in doing so I was careful to let my middle finger stick out in one of those characteristic "fuck you" gestures. Dammit! I felt good! Just like passing gas after a plate of red beans. I felt good! They might not have seen me clearly enough to make an issue out of it, but they at least thought I did something by the way they reacted briefly to my hand movement. I must confess that I did follow through by scratching the hell out of my head. This perhaps saved me from possible punishment.

But, at least I had struck back!

"My last offer, comrade," the lead interrogator kept up his

campaign against Evans. "Either you cooperate with us now or we simply cannot let you share hot meal. This opportunity may not come again. Just tell us, for example, how morale in your unit was before capture. What type guns you were using and if you had plenty ammunition. That's all, comrade. None of your answers can be said to help us. We just want to complete our records. Just tell us the answers to those simple questions, comrade, and you get chance to dig into this hot pork and rice with broth gravy. You blacks like plenty gravy, don't you comrade?"

"Yes suh, I always like plenty gravy. With lots of onions and garlic in it."

"Well, as you can tell, we do have plenty of onions in this broth gravy. Just smell for yourself, comrade." He then held the plate just under Evans' nose before placing it again on the table directly in front of him.

"Yes suh, it sho' smells good. But, I can't tell ya nuttin.' I can only tell ya me name, serial number and date of rank. I hopes y'all forgives me, suh. Please, kin I have one mouthful?" He wasn't educated and there was more than just a little bit of the Old South in him.

But, at this very moment Evans was the most beautiful and the most educated of the educated. I loved the guy. He had more guts in his ignorance and innocence than most of us with our intelligence . . . or presumed intelligence. Evans reminded me of countless rural dirt poor blacks who say what's really on their minds, regardless of any damn consequences. I have often said that the only free people were the so-called uneducated. The educated, especially some of my pompous friends, often appear preoccupied with being accepted by peers. They are forever careful to say things that please other people. They buy houses they can't afford, laugh when they really think the joke isn't silly, go along with any program just because it's the popular view, and praise the food when they really think it's lousy.

The so-called uneducated will tell you the truth for the most part. If they think the joke is silly, they usually will say so. If they think you are silly, they will say so. If they think the food is lousy, they simply won't eat it. They speak the truth and we call them stupid. The so-called educated tell pleasant lies and we say they have good manners, that they are socially acceptable. So, we, the educated, spend a lifetime trying to live the right lie in order to be socially accepted, to be a "Person of Breeding."

Evans desperately wanted a piece of pork and simply begged for it. I desperately wanted just to taste it but wouldn't dare ask. Begging was out of the question. I am what you might call a man of "breeding." It was important for me to be perceived as a proud macho black man. After all I was the top kick of Charlie Battery and was still respected as top in power. Hell! I was starving and I knew it. But, I consider myself educated and proper . . . so I acted the role. But, make no mistake, on a dark night in a deserted alley I probably would have mugged a person for a bit of pork in my state of deprivation. But, in front of my buddies, I didn't have the courage to beg for what I wanted while still refusing to give in to what our wily enemy wanted.

"Comrade," the main interrogator addressed Evans, "we like you. You man of the people. No 'fraid to ask like man. You good man, comrade, Good man." With that, they set the plate down in front of Evans who began devouring the contents like a mad animal. He didn't bother with the chopsticks. That would have slowed him. He tore into that plate with both hands.

"Y'll wants some?" he drawled. "Y'all wants some of dis?"

Before we could answer the main interrogator interrupted.

"No! Nothing for comrades! They not men! Only men eat. They starve! You eat, comrade, Eat."

Evans dug into the plate with fanaticism, seemingly bent on completing the meal before the two bastards changed their minds. I felt sick. God! I wanted just one damn bite of that pork. At one point in his haste, Evans dropped a piece of meat on the floor and I picked it up. The second interrogator quickly snatched it from me and placed it back on Evans' plate. Another two seconds and that particular piece would have been in my mouth. I chided myself for being so damn slow. I knew I was faster than that.

I just watched in admiration as Evans completed the plate. Here he was, uneducated and crude. But, he was eating hot pork and steaming rice . . . and he had not given up one iota of information to the enemy. Looking back, I now know that Evans was doing nothing more than his forefathers had done to survive slavery in the United States. He, in his ignorance, had employed old slave tactics to defeat a supposedly superior master. He had beaten them at their own game. There was no question that the enemy would have had to kill Evans in order to get him to divulge valuable information. He was simply too stoic in his perception of right and wrong. I loved the guy.

The Communists, as expected, made a production out of our departure from the interrogation. When we left the room, the Chinese cooks and the two interrogators tried their best to give the impression that we all had been having a delightful luncheon chat. The interrogators demanded that we shake their hands on the steps outside the room, in full view of the white POWs in the distance. The idea was to convey to our white counterparts that we, the blacks, had been most cooperative. Years later, back in the States, such tactics by the Communists would bring reaction from some whites who challenged the loyalty of black POWs. I must say this and say it emphatically, most blacks in POW camps are forever wary of being set up by the enemy, of having racial differences used against them. They quickly realize that any attempt by the enemy to "court them" is done to foster antagonism between blacks and whites in camp. Quite frankly, many whites, willing to believe anything negative about blacks, fall willing victims to this type of racial propaganda by the enemy. To be sure all black POWs understood this, we constantly reminded each other to be careful not to let any prison guard or officer cultivate any type friendship with us that might be misinterpreted. As Poppa Browne forever reminded us, "Boys, be friendly but not in anyway familiar with the little screw balls."

It must be stated clearly that the Communists also sought to use white POWs in the quest to plant seed of racial discord. They would secretly ask white POWs what they thought of us. Then, if a poor unsuspecting white "spoke off the record" about certain prejudices he had against blacks, the Communists would see to it that we eventually got not only what was said but exactly who made the statement.

# 5
# Forced Study Life and Communism

I have always concluded that there are three types of men: those that are street-wise, those that think they are street-wise but aren't, and those that are simply very naive. In any circumstance where groups of men are confined together for long periods of time, one has an occasion to come in contact with all three types.

I think this is particularly true of men in prison. It's amazing how brilliant some men are despite their limited formal education. Sergeant Willie Fields was such a man. He was also something else. Extremely bitter! Especially when it came to women. Born in rural Louisiana, he had somehow managed to lose all faith in the ability of women to remain loyal to one man. He was particularly outspoken when speaking about married women.

"Married women ain't worth a shit and I won't back down one inch from this position. Every married woman is one bedroom away from anotto man. I don't care what anyone says, I have it on good authority that they can't be trusted. I wouldn't marry another bitch if she was my ticket outta this goddamn place."

Speaking in that high pitched slow drawl, Sergeant Fields

would usually dominate the compound when it came to discussing women, black women in particular.

"I dunno nutin 'bout white women. Don't fool with 'em! I suspect they ain't a bit better 'n the caldonnas. Maybe worse 'cause they got mo' time to play. I'm talkin 'bout dem black bitches. The ones who say 'I do' to one man on a Sunday and 'I do' to his friend on Monday. Love 'em and leave 'em I say."

As a rule, Willie could always expect reaction from those who disagreed with him. To be sure, there were many who agreed. One of those who generally disagreed with Willie was Poppa Browne. To this day, I don't know whether Poppa Browne really disagreed with him or because he loved the challenge of debate with Willie.

Poppa Browne, as usual, would never lose his composure during these friendly confrontations. Willie, on the other hand, simply could not control his bitterness. He wouldn't debate, he would argue and he would get mad.

"I invited my best friend to my house to meet my family," Willie would re-tell an incident he had told us many times before, "and soon my wife start askin' me, 'when are you invitin' Roger over for dinner again? He seems like a nice fella.' When she asked about him three times in one month, I shoulda wised up then. No, not me. I was trusting. I was doing like the Good Book say, 'I think no evil.' In the meantime, this 'friend' was dusting my wife off at every turn. Damn goddamn bitches!"

"There you go again, Willie," Poppa Browne would usually chim in, "puttin down on all black women 'cause you had an unfortunate experience with one."

"What's so goddamn unfortunate 'bout it?" Willie would shoot back. "She wasn't the only one and I've told you that befo'."

"Okay, okay Willie, so you ran into two caldonnas who did you wrong. That's still no reason to point bad fingers at all the rest."

"Poppa Browne you're either gittin' old and forgitful or just absentminded." Willie was warming up now. The lecture was about to begin.

"There was this bitch called Della. Now Della and me had gone together for mo'n three years 'fore I went into service. Everybody knew we wuz gonna git married someday. I joins the service . . . decides to come home on furlough just to surprise her. I figured when she saw me she would go into fits or somethin' at seein' her baby home again. She went into fits all right. When I went to her pad and knocked on the door it took her forever to answer.

"That was the first mistake, Willie," Poppa Browne intervened. "When she didn't answer right away you shuda left and come back later. You were askin' for trouble. Why didn't you just leave, huh?"

"Leave? For what? For what goddammit? I heard the record player playin'. I knew Della was home! I thought maybe she was in the can or somethin' and I wanted to give her time to finish wiping her butt. When the bitch finally came to the door, her hair was all over her goddamn head and her eyes were as red as hell."

"They say when a bitch has red eyes some brother has really been puttin' it to her righteously, Willie," someone from the back yelled out in support.

"Amen," Willie acknowledged, "Amen! Then when I went into the room the 'funk' almost took my breath. One thing I have found out when two people have been screwin' in a hot room the room heat increases the smell of sex. Am I right or wrong?"

"You know damn well you're right Willie. The smell of a bitch in heat is a lot different than the smell of gumbo," someone shouted amid laughter.

"Damn right, Willie, you tell 'em what a stinkin' bitch smells like," someone volunteered. "Tell us 'bout the skunk, Willie."

Willie could always expect support from his friends. They would always provide the chorus, the affirmation he needed to shore up his position of bitterness.

"Then," Willie continued, "this dude walks out with a sheepish smile on his sweaty face. The couch was a mess. The room was so 'funky' until even the dude said 'it's kinda hot in here. I say screw all black ass bitches."

"You say 'screw all black ass bitches' 'cause what two or three sisters may have done to you. I say MAY 'cause they ain't here to defend themselves. We have only your word." Poppa Browne was unraveling that cool logic of his again.

"I don't give a you-know-what whether you believe me or not," fired back a very angry Willie Fields. "I done told ya what the bitches did to me and that's that!"

"You have accused those poor women of what you thought they were doing, Willie, but didcha at any time see either one of 'em goin' into or comin' out of a motel with their dudes? Didcha, Huh? Talk to me now."

"Look, lemme tell y'all cock suckers somethin' 'bout women. Y'all ain't gotta wait for 'em to walk outta no damn motel room. They tip thar hands long 'fore then."

"Preach on Brother Willie."

"I mean when a woman has hots for a man," Willie continued, "she has many ways to give 'im the message."

"Talk to us, Willie! Aw, whip it on us!"

Willie was boiling over now. He was up to the challenge.

"I saw my ex-wife once shake hands with one of my closest friends."

"That's who really do it to you Willie."

"Now for Heavens sake you're gonna tell us yo' wife used to bed down with any yo' friends she shook hands with," Poppa Browne chimed in rather sarcastically.

"Damn near!" Willie shot back. "Damn near! The point is, when she finished the hand shake she just didn't let go. Uh no. No siree. That bitch sorta let her hands slowly slide off his 'uns. At the same time she looked him dead in the eyes, as if to say, 'got the message?' I saw the filthy ass bitch. She didn't think I saw her but I did."

"What you actually saw, Willie," Poppa Browne shot to the attack, as cooly as ever, "was what you wanted to see. Yo' po' wife, man, I tell ya, she never had a chance."

"The hell you say!" Willie shot back with ever increasing bitterness. "When I told her 'bout what I saw she said the same thing you just said, "Willie, you'se seein' things you wanta see. I just shook the man's hand and now you got me in bed with 'em. Damn, Willie, I don't want dat man.' The lying bitch!"

"Why in Heaven's names does she have to be a 'lyin bitch' Willie? Is it possible she just might have told ya the truth?"

"Poppa Browne, that woman wasn't no goddamn where near the truth. They wasn't even on the same block! Y'all know as well as me that when ya catch a bitch in a lie she starts cryin' like a goddamn dog. I used to be taken in by that. But no mo! Not me! The bitch!"

"Willie, how long were you married?" Poppa Browne calmly asked.

"The foist time I stayed married six years too long."

"And the second time, Willie?"

"The second time I hung in thar nine years too long. Why?"

"You were a married man a total of fifteen years, huh?"

"Yeah? Fifteen goddamn lousy, miserable years. Puttin' both of 'em bitches together I betcha I couldn't squeeze one good year of being married."

"Wait, now, come on, Willie, I'm tryin' to gitcha to think."

"For what? I knows what I done lived. I jes have to remember it. Ain't nuttin' to think about!"

"You tell 'em, Willie, You tell 'em. Hey, man, when a dude's been burnt once before he knows fire's hot. He ain't gotta think about it."

Willie's legions were usually very vocal in their support.

"Damn right!" Willie bristled, gloating a bit at what he considered a point well made.

"You were married a total of fifteen years . . ." Poppa Browne continued.

"Fifteen goddamn years," Willie interrupted, "thar's a difference!"

"Okay, whatever," Poppa Browne agreed. "Now are you tellin' me that in all that time you never once visited the bedroom of another woman? Is that what you want me to believe, huh, Willie?"

"I ain't wantin' you to believe nuttin'. If I did step out every now and then I sho' as hell kept it a long way from my wife. I at least 'spected her enough not to do anythin' in front of her, or to make like I wuz wantin' to screw one of her friends. Thar was a time that last bitch of mine wud ask four, five times in one week 'bout one of my friends, wantin' to know if he wud show up at a given function or not. I honestly believe the bitch was so hung up 'till she didn't realize herself how many times she was asking 'bout the dude."

"Willie, Willie, Willie, you gotta problem."

"Sure I have," Willie quipped. "I don't trust married women, especially the holier-than-thou ones. My foist wife claimed to be such a helluva church worker. Shit! One Sunday I noticed her looking quite hard at one of the ushers. I mean the bitch kept watching him outta side her eyes. I made out like I was busy listenin' to the sermon. After church we wuz talking to some friends when that usher dude walks by. Yu shuda seen my wife breakin' her eyes trying' to get a look at the bastard. When I got home and mentioned what I saw, she went off, sayin' I was accusin' her again. The lyin' bitch! I'm sittin' thar lookin' at her hawk the dude and she has the goddamn nerve to deny it. I shuda killed the low down cheatin' dog."

"Shuda kicked her ass, Willie. That's what you oughta done baby boy. Kicked her assss!"

Usually when this type of camp debate occurred, my thoughts inevitably turned to my Florence. She wouldn't be human if she didn't feel the sensation of loneliness. Hell, I was lonely too. It was a bit easier for me because there was no woman around to provide temptation. I could afford to be true, pious, loyal and all of that other bullshit. The truth of the matter is that my thoughts were too preoccupied with surviving to deal even remotely with sex. But, listening to Willie, should I doubt Florence? I would be terribly dishonest if I said I didn't consider the possibility that some other man, possibly a 'best friend' was enjoying the fruits of my Florence. Not that I would ever doubt her love, I never have. But, human emotions are funny. They certainly make us unpredictable. Regardless of the best of intentions, we will all yield given the right set of circumstances. I remembered well the times I found myself in bed with married women who perhaps had sworn to their husbands they would never bed down with another man. But they still did . . . lots of times, promising at each encounter that it would be the final time. But, it wasn't.

With Florence, I suppose the difference was that I knew her. Florence was very proud, too proud I always concluded, to give some other man the satisfaction of boasting that he had "ripped off old Thompson's wife." Deep in the heart, however, I knew there was always that outside possibility. That right moment. That right man. That sexual fantasy that became all too real. Could happen. But, I was still inclined to doubt it. Then, too, what in the hell could I do about it locked up in a stinking prisoner of war camp somewhere in North Korea? I had to face still another reality: if Florence were locked up in North Korea and I was roaming around on the streets, would I be pure? Frankly, I wouldn't bet a pack of cigarettes on my chastity over a haul. It's not that I am weak. Quite the contrary. It's just that I like a good piece of tail every now and then. Still, the very fact of Florence ever making love to another man, and enjoying it, would have been too much. I simply could not take it.

Men fully expect women to forgive them for being unfaithful. Yet, with few exceptions, men never really forgive wives they know to have been unfaithful. Men in the camp generally agreed that they could not in good conscience ever respect or trust their wives again if they discovered them in bed with another man. I often thought about my own attitude on the issue and concluded that on this point I too shared the consensus.

I think the reason is fairly easy to understand, at least to me. Men don't have to be in love to make love. That's why we can take a prostitute without even knowing her name. With women, with few exceptions, sex comes harder when there is no emotion involved. Sure, there are women who are physically attracted to men initially. The woman may have even fantasized sexually about them. But, when the moment of truth arrives, the woman usually holds out until she is a bit more sure of herself emotionally. Now, I am in no way a sex expert. Far from it. But, usually when a woman engages in sex, the man means something to her. This is the very fact that drives husbands up the walls. They know this too. This fact alone dramatically points out the husband's gross insecurity. I should say our gross insecurity. This is, I believe, one reason we as men find it harder to forgive, because we know that more than sex was involved. The more I think of us as men, when it comes to women, the more I conclude that we are all a bunch of thankless bastards.

# 6
# Brainwashing

Our formal indoctrination came in the form of so-called "study periods." The enemy's objective was very simple: to convert us to Communism. I must in all candor say that most of us were simply not prepared for these "study periods." They were mental torture. The sessions were extremely well organized. First, we were divided into five-member study groups. The Communists then requested each group to select one person who would serve as monitor for that group.

The instructions to the monitors were sharp, clear and to the point. Each monitor had to record, on paper, everything his particular group discussed during the daily study period. Nothing could be left out. The monitor's notes had to include not only what was discussed, but who discussed it. All monitors were also ordered to turn their daily notes into headquarters for "evaluation." We later found out that "evaluation" really meant dealing with any "wise-ass" identified by a monitor's daily notes.

Sergeant Willie Fields was assigned to my little group. I realized the minute he was assigned that things would be different, quite lively. I only hoped it would not be dangerous. Willie was just too damn argumentative in a situation that called for tact and long moments of silence. You simply don't shout back at a man who has a gun stuck in your guts. You don't, of course, unless you are a Willie Fields. Now, I am one of those strange fellows who believes in living and let live. You do your thing and I'll damn sure do mine. In our situation, however, Willie's outspoken lifestyle was pretty dangerous to my continued good health and I knew it.

One of the main instructors for our study sessions was a little half-pint Chinese whom we secretly called "Chop Suey." He always had somewhat of a chicken shit half-smile on his face. It was hard to tell when he was actually angry. I've always been most aware of people who could slit your throat without any show of emotion. Chop Suey was, in my opinion, such a person.

In addition to imparting words of wisdom about Communism, Chop Suey would casually roam from one study group to another, smiling, and, occasionally, asking a question to ascertain some response that might indicate an attitude. I didn't trust that little fellow one iota. He was too polite. For the most part, however, he let each study group conduct its own session. After all, there was a monitor who would later report what was discussed.

Back to the monitor. To be sure, no one in his right mind wanted to be selected a group monitor. This was akin to having your mother-in-law ask you to judge the daughter. No way you can win! At best, survival in this circumstance depended on the ability of the monitor to exercise extreme discretion in his note taking. He had to know when to lie, when to tell the truth and when to be "faulty" with his memory. Inherent in all this was an unusual paradox. If the monitor "doctored" his notes to conceal what was actually said, he did so at great personal risk. The Communists had a habit of randomly selecting a POW from one of the groups and asking him to repeat what had actually been said in that day's study session. If there were discrepancies between the monitor's notes and what the unsuspecting POW related, then the monitor's butt was in a sling. On the other hand, the unsuspecting POW could abruptly change his own story, lie like a dog, and say the monitor's recollections were more accurate. If the Commies bought this, the monitor was home free. But, the POW's butt was now in a sling. No-win situation was possible

Since we quickly found out that the Communists were employing a system of "checks and balances" as related to the study periods, it became imperative for the monitor and group members to coordinate their lies. Our little group hastily developed a system for helping our monitor lie for us for the record. Since Chop Suey roamed from one group to another, we had to be subtle in the manner by which "we got our lies together." A typical exchange among us went something like this:

> "America, despite its apparent preoccupation with racial intolerance," one politically insensitive POW might say rather boldly, "is still the only country in the world where a poor black man from the cotton fields can become a millionaire, given a bit of luck. Under Communism, he ain't gonna have nothin!"

Obviously if the monitor reported these exact words the POW who made them would no doubt be called in for questioning. To help him "correct himself for the record" the POW monitor might repeat the statement for the record in the following edited manner:

> "In other words, you're saying America might be best for a poor black cotton picker who desires riches above all else, while Communism might be more appealing to him who wishes only to live simply, sharing with neighbors any good fortunes . . .?"

> "Er . . . uh huh . . . er . . . yeah!" might be the response if the group member agreed to the monitor's edited version, the one he intended to insert in the records.

With this system, it really didn't matter if the monitor and the group member were called in separately. They now could at least be consistent with their lies as to what was actually said in any given group session. I can imagine that this type survival "double talk" went on during the days of slavery as our forefathers talked "under", "around" and "over the heads" of unsuspecting slave masters. Survival actions have always been a staple among blacks. We learn it early. We have to! I've always contended that any twelve-year-old black boy from the ghetto is more capable of surviving in the streets, without a dime, than a white college professor from Yale who graduated at the head of his class. The fellow from Yale was taught by teachers. That ghetto youngster was schooled by life. If you flunk the course at Yale you simply don't graduate. You flunk in the ghetto and you lose your goddamn life. The bottom lines are different. No time for fun and games in the ghetto. It's all business.

Even with our makeshift communication system there were flaws. Our system was far from fail-safe. If, as an example, Chop Suey decided to linger while visiting our particular discussion group, our monitor had to make damn sure his notes were accurate. No "editing" of any discussion overheard personally by Chop Suey. We all understood that under such circumstances we were on our own. It was then up to each man to "edit" himself very carefully. When Chop Suey was around, the word was "speak slowly and carefully . . . know what you're going to say before it comes out or it might be your ass."

Then, too, the Communists had another way of getting to us, psychologically. They would call one of us in and suggest that our monitor had included certain inflammatory things in his notes. Things, according to them, for which we could be punished, even brought to trial. We knew they were lying. Still this did cause some tension between the monitor and group members. I will say this, the Commies were artisans at planting seeds of discord.

Looking back, I guess the reason they wanted some friction

between the POW monitor and his group was to preclude too much collaboration on the notes. We soon realized what was happening and made a conscious effort to ignore their games of "seed planting." I won't say we always succeeded, but we made a conscious effort. Sometimes making a conscious effort isn't worth a damn. One can make a conscious effort to ignore the pains of hunger. But, the more you try to consciously ignore a problem, the more pronounced the problem becomes. We, to the man, knew our monitor would never "willingly" fink on us. What we didn't know were the limits of his endurance. We all have our breaking point. To be sure, the job of a POW monitor was a no-win situation from beginning to end. Being selected was similar in many respects to being indicted for something you didn't do.

It was against this hostile background that we selected a reluctant Sergeant Freddie Anderson to be the monitor for our particular group. Freddie was a quiet spoken, mild mannered sergeant from Houston, Texas. Alert and philosophical, he was cut from the Poppa Browne mold. A career soldier, he was in his early thirties, lean and tall, and prematurely bald. He had this scholarly presence about him. I remember well his only reaction after we had selected him monitor:

"Fellas, don't make what's gonna be a miserable job an impossible one. Y'all knows the situation I'm now in. So, I'll need yo' cooperation and understanding. Won't be able to fight y'all and the enemy too."

As might be expected, Freddie encountered more than a little difficulty in trying to save Willie Fields from himself. Regardless, I thought Freddie handled him better than most. The man had incredible patience and restraint during his "study period" confrontations with Willie, and there were many. Willie was simply one argumentative bastard. I remember one occasion when Willie simply refused to let Freddie "edit" his comment.

"I ain't got no trust 'n' faith in no kinda government what takes parta my hard earned money and gives it to my no-account neighbors. None! That's a buncha crap! I don't care what y'all say, I ain't got no kinda hard on for Communism. None!"

"Willie," I remember Freddie calmly trying to edit this uncontrollable bastard, "you mean that you are concerned that in an effort to spread the wealth, Communism seems to great personal initiative . . ."

"Naw, naw, naw," Willie shot back, "that aint what I mean. I means just what I don already said.   No ifs, buts, or maybes 'bout it. Communism . . . ain't . . . got . . . SHIT . . . for Willie Fields! Nuttin'! Tell 'em just like I said it, Freddie. Don't matter to me. I ain't scared of these people. Not me!"

A week later Willie spent two days and nights sitting on a log. Even out there on that log alone, he remained "defiance personified." He had a way of squatting on that log, arms folded with both of his trousers rolled up knee high. His butt rested partially over the rear of the log as if he were back home in an outhouse taking a leisurely crap. I doubt if the Communists could ever break Willie's spirits. I suspected the reason they didn't come down on him harder was because they simply considered him crazy.

Back to the indoctrination, an incident arose during one of our study periods that I shall never forget, primarily because it spoke so well of what, potentially, could happen in America today . . . nearly 38 years later.

Chop Suey was lecturing to us about the infamous Boxer Rebellion . . . one in which the Chinese attempted to oust the British from colonial control. I also remember that I could care less than a damn about the Boxer Rebellion. I cared even less about anything Chop Suey or anyone else said about a Boxer Rebellion. Hell, I wanted to go home, period. Still, Chop Suey droned on about that rebellion.

"Chief reason we Chinese failed to reach our objective," I recall him saying, "was because of drugs and dope. Nothing else. Drugs and dope defeated us . . . not the enemy. We beat ourselves. Not British!"

# True Colors

I remember Chop Suey pausing for a moment, in a reflective mood, as if really lamenting the defeat at the hands of the British.

"Same thing will happen in America," he continued.

"You see. You see. First drugs will rip through your universities and colleges. It will destroy minds of bright students. You see. You see. Then, drugs and dope will reach down into the secondary schools. When that happen . . . and it will . . . your America will experience a revolution. Kids will rise up against authority. You see. You see."

Nearly thirty eight years later, I would remember Chop Suey's prophetic words as I read news accounts of the youth gang drug related killings in Los Angeles, Miami, New York and of course, my home town, Detroit, the murder capital.

Thirty eight years later I would personally become involved in a drug education campaign in an effort to preclude from happening in the United States what actually occurred years ago (mid 1800-1900) in China.

Thirty eight years later, in the twilight of my life, I would find myself again fighting Chop Suey, trying to make sure his words would not eventually be the ultimate reality for this nation's destiny.

At the time Chop Suey was lecturing, Willie kept squirming restlessly in his seat. He, too, couldn't care less. Finally, out of frustration, nothing more, Willie shot back.

"Wait a minute, Comrade," Willie began in that irritated manner, "jes hold on a minute, suh. Now, I came from the South. Born 'n' raised thar. We ain't nevah gonna have no mo' revolutions in America. I kin tell ya dat. No mo'. Believe me! No one knows America bettern us Americans."

Chop Suey walked over closer to Willie and continued in a patronizing manner.

"We Chinese failed to believe it would happen to us, Comrade, but it did. History has already documented that fact."

"I don't care what history said," Willie retorted.

"I jes done told ya what AINT GONNA happen in America.

No ways!"

Chop Suey never raised his voice. He was a cool bastard.

"When it happens someday, Comrade, remember that we warned you. Drugs and dope will destroy your country someday. You see."

'Ya tryin' to tell me we'se gonna have a revolution?"

Willie asked quietly, surprising the rest of us by his sudden softness.

"Let's just say it'll be a little small overthrow," Chop Suey concluded, now breaking out in a sheepish smile.

Years later I would remember those words as I read account after account of runaway drug problems in the various learning institutions across the nation. Was that little smiling idiot right? Did he know something we didn't? With kids killing parents and other family members during drug induced rages, who's to say that little smiling bastard back in North Korea was wrong. I can only hope like hell he was. But . . . still the grim realities are printed daily in the newspapers. Like it or not . . . America's drug problem is indeed an acute problem for which there appears no immediate solutions. Let's just hope that little smiling idiot was wrong in his prophecy. Whether he was wrong or not, consider that too many of our fine U.S. military men today are using drugs at alarming proportions. Consider that drug use during the Viet Nam war was outrageously high. Consider that many servicemen aboard ships today are reportedly experiencing too many drug related incidents of violence. If all of these are not true, then we can no longer rely on reports of the news media.

# 7
# Camp Elections

During the early stages of our imprisonment, the Chinese had quartered all black POWs together, regardless of rank. Racism had absolutely nothing to do with it. It had everything to do with propaganda . . . and we blacks knew it. We understood full well that white POWs suspected that we, if given the chance, would cooperate with the enemy. The Chinese also knew that isolating us from the whites would only further inflame white suspicions. Some whites also felt that we were being separated so the Chinese could treat us better. Bullshit! We were starving and getting our butts kicked just as much, if not more, than the whites. In my opinion, many white American POWs were on "guilt trips." They didn't have to be reminded that as a race we were always treated poorly back home. Some white POWs apparently felt we might take advantage of the situation "to get even." Make no mistake, the Commies seized every opportunity to aggravate white suspicions. They also wasted little time pointing out to us that white America, not Communism, was our chief enemy.

To be sure, the Commies had separated us for the sole purpose of "special indoctrination." They apparently felt their chances for implanting political bullshit in us would be better if they kept us apart.

The whites went to great lengths to convince us their concerns for us were legit. They were quite enthusiastic in demanding that the Commies quarter black NCOs "according to the privileges of rank."

A few black POWs quickly joined the chorus. But, the overwhelming majority of us simply didn't give a damn. Personally, I wasn't interested in going elsewhere in a damn prison compound. To hell with that! I wanted to go home. Then, too, I was more than a little irritated that the white NCOs were demanding that we black NCOs be quartered with them. I guess I knew damn well that these same "concerned whites" would be the first to demand our ouster from their neighborhoods back home. But, in North Korea in 1951, '52 and '53 they needed us very close to them. Very close! Not because of love, mind you, but because of a need to "keep an eye on us." Looking back, after all these years I sometimes wonder why we black NCOs didn't bitch more to stay where we were. I had no problems at all being quartered with the other black enlisted men. None! I guess one reason we never bitched about this issue was because it really wasn't a priority with us. Sure, if the Commies had been feeding us steak and eggs, bedding us down in queen-sized beds, and providing us with maid service, we may have bitched like all hell to stay put. But, parched corn is parched corn no matter where you eat it. A body filled with lice is a body filled with lice no matter where that body beds down. So, moving in with a bunch of white NCOs in the same compound in 1951 was not a priority with a group of homesick, starving black POWs. No way! Our priorities were lack of food—lice—loneliness—and the ever present prospects of death.

Finally, amid ever-growing complaints from whites, all the black NCOs were moved to a regular NCO company, one consisting of 40 blacks and about 360 whites. The Commies, ever on the alert, even took advantage of our move to new quarters to garner cannon fodder for more propaganda.

"Bop Daddy" gathered all the black and white NCOs outside headquarters and explained the new camp structure.

"Here," this forever little 'dapper dan' began, "we all family. Must live like family. Every company will have minorities. It's the people's way. We make no difference! That's imperialist way. Your way!"

"Bop Daddy" failed to mention that whites had demanded the integration of NCOs. He would have us believe it was all Communist inspired. At the time the black and white NCOs were integrated into one company, Sergeant Freddie Anderson was serving more or less as spokesman and monitor for all black NCOs. This was in addition to his chores as our "study group" monitor. Fred had also managed to gain some measure of respect from the Chinese. The Chinese had further evidenced their respect by recognizing him as "senior camp advisor." Although there were several "camp advisors" who met regularly with the Commies, Fred was unofficially looked upon as "top dog." To be sure, and as expected, Fred's stature triggered some quiet reaction from the whites. No one in his right mind wished to antagonize the Chinese. Those people were simply too unpredictable . . . too damn dangerous! Fred's problems with the white POWs while at camp were minor as compared to the problems he would encounter later upon return to the United States. He was destined to be called everything from "collaborator," "traitor," "turn-coat," "black smith," to you name it. All this for trying to keep the Commies off the asses of white and blacks alike.

Forgive me if I sound like a five-and-dime store radical, but whites, especially American whites, cannot bring themselves to realistically accept black leadership. I don't care how hard they try or whatever the circumstances, they simply cannot! This lack of black leadership acceptance by whites is too imbedded in their character. Few whites in the United States of America want blacks making decisions for them. As a rule, with varying exceptions, the few blacks who manage to reach high political posts usually do so because they come primarily from black districts. When black police officers were first recruited in the South, they were recruited only to arrest fellow blacks . . . not whites and damn sure no white women! On the other hand, white Southern police officers could arrest anyone and, as a rule, came down particularly hard on blacks. A small wonder that a black child coming out of such an environment had anything but a good self-image of himself. If one understands the social order as it existed in this country, especially in the South in the 50's, then one can readily understand that the white POWs in North Korea in the 50's easily resented a black sergeant Fred Anderson making decisions for them, decisions that might well affect their lives. But, again, with a bunch of little midgets with guns running around all over the place, the white POWs had little to say about the predicament then. They did later, however.

The white POWs "tolerated" Fred as top camp POW advisor simply because they had no choice. Generally, they were courteous and gave him little lip. Again, they had no choice. But, one would have to be a moron not to sense a basic distaste among them that a black was making policy decisions that affected their daily lives.

Keep in mind that Fred had been selected by the Chinese to be senior camp advisor . . . not by the camp POWs. His eventual selection by the entire camp, including whites, came during a series of camp elections called by the Commies. The purpose of the elections was to select official camp representatives who would make up a so-called "camp council." This would be the official body that dealt with the Chinese and North Koreans on our behalf.

When nominations for candidates were first offered, not one black was nominated. Camp Commander "Bop Daddy" chided the whites saying, in effect, "This not like your country. Everybody should have representation. Why you no give your black comrades at least a chance to run for election?"

It was at this point that we, the blacks, nominated Fred as a candidate for a possible seat on the official council. His nomination was unanimous! It must be kept in mind that although whites voted for his nomination, they did so with virtually a gun at their backs. They knew the Commies were not going to allow any elections without at least some blacks among the candidates. It must be fully understood also that the role of the Commies was again motivated by propaganda. They knew exactly what they were doing, forever planting seeds of discord, the old divide and conquer routine.

When the election campaign got underway, each candidate was permitted to go from one company to another in an attempt to state his case. Each related what they intended to do, for example, to improve camp conditions, to foster better communications with our captors, to state our case with dignity and courage, etc. Some of the candidates were quite adept at stating their cases. One white sergeant was extremely convincing. The campaign generated some much needed recreational type activity around the compound. The Commies even permitted the candidates to paint placards and place them in strategic spots. In a word, the campaign was quite lively. But, in the end it was Sergeant Fred Anderson who won by a landslide as chief camp spokesman . . . for whites and blacks! As stated earlier, this selection was to prove a disaster for him later on upon return to the States.

# 8
# Solitary Confinement

Keep in mind that we had been secretly informed as early as 1951 that the Commies were monitoring our mail. We knew this but were still inclined to "let it all hang out" when writing to our wives and loved ones. A man in confinement has a great need to communicate his feeling to someone on the outside. He is driven by this need. I didn't give a damn if the Chinese read my letters as long as they eventually got to Florence. Then, too, since the Commies didn't make a daily, weekly or monthly thing about our letters, we tended to forget that this too was all part of the plan . . . to "lull us into being careless." I remember well being called in for another "routine" review of my camp conduct. As pointed out earlier, the Commies did this about once every two months. During these "routine" reviews, the Commies pulled your records and related the things they knew about you . . . the new things . . . things they found out were more or less contained in letters they had monitored. On this particular occasion, they told me my wife had purchased a new Chevrolet . . . that she was now teaching school . . . that my uncle was now in politics. They also took this occasion to lash into me personally, telling me I had knowledge that could be put to use helping my people but that I wasn't doing a damn thing but wasting it. They suggested that my lazy attitude was nothing but a total disgrace to my people, to the black race in particular, and to Third World Peoples in general. This "lecture" really got under my collar. I guess it wasn't so much what they said as how they said it. It was said in a very condescending manner. I hate people to talk to me in a condescending manner, always did. Reminded me of too many well meaning patronizing whites back home in Arkansas. The Commies really ticked me off during this particular session. What's more, I overacted!

For lack of better sense, I shouted at my interrogators, telling them I was forever tired of their reminding me of my problems but never offering any realistic solutions. I told them I knew my wife had a Chevrolet . . . that she was now making $4000 a year . . . that I, too, was making $5000 a year! I challenged them to help her make $10,000 a year . . . me $15,000 and give us a Cadillac and I then might be interested in listening to them. For a moment, the two interrogators looked at me in stunned silence, as if to say, "this black fellow is crazy." I felt good after that blast. It had been building up and now I had released it. Anger does give birth to false bravery. Now that I had gotten it off my chest, I now wondered what these little monsters would do to me. For a brief instance, I wanted to reach out and eat my words.

One of the interrogators finally rose slowly. This little roly-poly fellow was angry. His face was flushed with anger. A fool could see it.

"You stupid capitalist!" he began. "No good stupid capitalist! You come here . . . with capitalist arrogance while blood of our people on your filthy hands!"

With this he knocked the hell out of me. I fell to the floor, expecting a kick at any moment. In fact, I braced myself for a kick. These little monsters believed in kicking. They loved planting their foot in your stomach or groin, especially in the groin.

Unaccountably, the interrogators didn't hit or kick me

again. They merely helped me up and walked me back to my company. I was thankful for no heavy punishment. But, I was also concerned. These people didn't forget much. I was sure I would hear of my outburst later. But for the time being, I was glad to be out of that room.

I quickly noted that little incident in the little Red Book the Commies had given us. There was a standing order against any diary of any type. The Chinese actually wanted us to make notes in those Red Books about what we learned about Communism. I had begun using it as a convenient vehicle for maintaining my diary. Even if I were forced to burn it, the mental impression of what I had written would not be easily forgotten. We had been warned by both Sergeants Browne and Anderson not to include things that might mean our death if the diary were ever found. We had been warned repeatedly about this. However, I couldn't resist the temptation.

I recorded things such as our "super ability to prepare for the Korean battles." I also mentioned, in fact bragged about the ability of U.S. troops to eat turkey on Thanksgiving. I recorded how U.S. fighting men always got their mail on time, no matter how bitter the conditions of the battlefield. I made it a point to document my observations of the long trek to the prison compound. I didn't ever want to forget that bit of human suffering and dying. I even included the fact that some POWs were on the borderline of collaborating with the enemy. I foolishly mentioned three names, one of whom was black. I was really pouring out my guts in that little Red Book.

I was not discreet at all. Then, again, I never really figured on getting caught. No poor slob enters into an illegal act with the idea of getting caught. No one! To be sure, many of us kept diaries. To be even more sure, none of us expected to be caught.

The discovery came rather accidentally. The Commies, apparently suspecting that some of us were planning an escape, decided to make an unscheduled inspection of all quarters. They came in one morning, shouting, ordering all of us to strip down then hustle outside. I can still hear them barking their commands:

"Clothes off! Move! Outside! All clothes off! Now! Run outside! Move! Move!"

The confusion was about as one might expect it to be as grown men quickly shed clothes and run outside, not knowing what to expect once they get outside.

We stood outside for about an hour as the guards went on a rampage inside our quarters. We could hear them throwing things around and shouting words we had no way of interpreting. Later, when they completed the ransacking and permitted us to go back inside, I discovered that, among other things, my Red Book was missing! I nearly panicked!

Although I knew they had taken my diary, the Commies didn't move on me immediately. Knowing them, I guess they wanted me to stew in the uncertainty of my fate. Obviously, I feared the worst. Several diaries were taken . . . but no one was called in immediately. But, you can bet we were all dying a slow mental death daily, not knowing what the enemy was cooking up for us.

Finally, about nine months later, it happened! I was taken to headquarters one morning to see "Bop Daddy." Contrary to my apprehensions, it wasn't a rough or long session. This little Dapper Dan was quite direct and brief:

"We have discovered, Comrade, that you are quite confused about a lot of things. Too many things. You need time to meditate, to organize your thoughts better. We take you place you can do this. You confused man."

Not only was I a confused man, I was a frightened man! I didn't like the tone of his voice. He was absolutely too casual about it all. He was like a minister saying the last rites to a condemned man.

Two guards then walked me through several camps until we reached a rather isolated area. One can imagine the thoughts racing through my mind. I recalled how the Germans and the

Japanese had hustled victims off during World War II and executed them. I had fully resolved not to die a helpless dog.

If they attempted to stand me up alongside a tree to shoot me they would do so only after a bitter struggle. My hands were not tied so I knew I could make a last-ditch effort to defend myself, regardless of the odds.

As it turned out, the guards took me to a small sunken hut that I quickly realized was some type of isolation chamber. I was pushed down inside the dark, damp and hot hut. It was July, 1952 and the weather was searing. There were no windows, only cracks through which a measure of air could drift. Then, too, the place had a repugnant odor! As I moved around I soon realized why. Apparently several POWs who were detained there earlier had defacated all over the place and no one had bothered to clean things up. The stench caused me to vomit immediately, adding still another bit of odor to the existing stench.

I shed my clothing and tied them around my body. Didn't dare lay them in all the filth. The place was not high enough for me to stand so I squatted. Poppa Browne had always told us never to panic during a crisis. He reminded us that to do so would only aggravate the situation. He advised us to pause, gather our thoughts, and commence logically. I decided to do exactly that, if I could. God! The place was hot . . . and it stunk! After a fashion, I concluded that one thing had to go and go without delay! The odor.

Since the earth flooring was damp, I began digging.

I then began to push the body waste into the small excavations, covering it quickly. It must have taken me an hour to bury all the stuff. But, I finally got the job done, feeling rather proud that I was remaining cool during the crisis. I remember taking my shirt and trousers and fanning the air, trying to force more of the odor of stench through the cracks. I then spread the clothing on the floor and more of less collapsed from the combination of stifling heat and near exhaustion.

"Whatever y'all do, don't panic during any kinda crisis."

Poppa Browne's words were now my rallying cry. Whatever else, in my predicament I had to keep my focus. I had to know exactly what I was doing at all times . . . and I had to make sense. Although the heat, stench, and cramped quarters were challenging enough, my real fear was claustrophobia. I have always feared being locked in any uncomfortable place from which I could not free myself. I was stuck in an elevator for several hours once and nearly died from fright. The combined feeling of helplessness and danger plays havoc with one's mind. I was told that during World War II the Germans would tie a prisoner's hands behind his back, blindfold him, and suspend him by the feet for more than ten hours at a time. The idea of having my hands tied behind my back and upside down body suspended ten feet above the ground was, to me, a torture worse than death.

Now, here I was, locked in a cell in which I could not stand, could hardly breathe, could barely see outside, with no idea how long the confinement was going to last. If they had told me I would be confined for, say, ten days I could play mental games to "mark time." But, the Commies gave me no reference point and quite frankly I was afraid.

After about fifteen hours in the cramped cell, I really had to fight an encroaching panic created by my inability to stand. Amazing how we humans take simple things for granted in this life.

In order to combat the rising fear, I began to repeat aloud Poppa Browne's advice.

"Whatever y'all do, don't panic during any kinda crisis."

I had to remain calm . . . and in control. Slowly, I began to do some floor exercises trying to ignore the heat. I then tried to remember others who suffered more. I especially remembered stories I had heard about the dreaded Angola prison in Louisiana. I was told that sadistic guards in the death house would amuse themselves by abruptly awakening prisoners late at night and shouting that it was their time to go to the electric chair. I was told how the redneck guards got a good laugh out of such inhumane antics, especially since the inmates were mostly black.

On about the fifth day, I found a peculiar strength in an old spiritual that I had sung so many times as a child. I would start singing it each time I felt my resolve weakening:

"Rock of ages, cleft for me, let me hide my-self in thee; Let the wa-ter and the blood, From my wound-ed side which flowed . . ."

I wasn't born during slavery, but I can now say with great confidence that I know the strength the slaves got from those great spirituals:

". . . be of sin the dou-ble cure, Save from wrath and make me pure. Could my tears forev-er flow, could my zeal no languor know, these for sin could not a-tone; Thou must save, and thou a-lone. . ."

I recalled that little rural church in Arkansas where my parents and friends droned seemingly forever on that song. Although I had always like it, it never really caught on with me until that period in North Korea in 1952. I needed a crutch that wouldn't fail and it didn't. Looking back, I now realize that I had only called upon the same crutches that my forefathers had used. When they sang it, they meant it. When I sang it in that stinking hole in 1952. I knew quite well that my entire soul went into it. I was a frightened man, alone with my spiritual self and the warm tears bathing my dark face:

". . . In my hand no price I bring; Sim-ply to thy cross I cling. While I draw this fleet-ing breath, When my eyes shall close in death, When I rise to worlds un-known, And be-hold thee on they throne, Rock of A-ges cleft for me, Let me hide my-self in thee."

The old folks used to say there is power in prayer and in singing "The Lord's songs." The fact that my salvation in 1952 rested so heavily on one song makes me the last person to ever again doubt the wisdom of the old folks.

". . . In my hand no price I bring, Sim-ply to thy cross I cling .

Two weeks after I had been placed in the hole I was taken out. Weak, starving, and nearly blinded by the abrupt return to sunlight, I had survived! Didn't matter that this tall lanky Arkansas farm boy was nearly dead, the important thing was that I was still breathing.

I was led back to headquarters to face "Bop Daddy". When I entered the room I nearly fell to the floor. I barely had enough strength to support the bones that were now my legs.

"Having problems, comrade?" "Bop Daddy" asked in a casual 'I don't give a damn if you die' manner.

"Not really." I lied, trying to sound every bit as casual as he but failing miserably.

He stared in the mirror momentarily then turned toward me, a sheepish smile slowly becoming evident.

"Tell me, Comrade Thompson, anyone disturb your meditation, huh?"

He was playing with me and I was in no mood to be toyed with on this particular day.

"No . . . everything was just fine," I again lied.

At this particular point in time I would have given up Florence for just five minutes in a dark alley with "Bop Daddy."

"Keep in mind, comrade, your place in hole reserved. Whenever we feel you need more time to think over things you go back. Understand?"

"Yes. I understand."

The rage within me was almost uncontrollable. Perhaps the only thing that prevented me from saying something stupid as a parting shot was the unforgettable memory of my ordeal. I didn't want to return to that hole under any circumstances. Another two weeks in that thing and they would have dragged out a corpse.

"You may return, comrade," came the dismissal order from "Bop Daddy", again patting his hair in front of the mirror.

I returned to my quarters vowing never to forget my ordeal or to get involved in any circumstances that might result in a repeat performance. At that point I was just a bit broken and I knew it. It would take me several weeks to readjust physically and mentally.

# 9
# An Uppity Smart Ass

Several months passed without incident after my ordeal in solitary confinement. I had gone to great pains to stay clear of trouble. I knew that my "attitude" and the discovery of my diary had made me a marked man. I had to be careful.

All of us, however, are trapped by our personality. No matter how hard I tried, I seemed to have come across to the Communists as a wise guy. I really wasn't. It was just my personality to be outspoken about certain things.

Another crisis generated by my personality came during one of our study periods. I had been asked by Chop Suey to relate something I knew about history. Of all the topics, I decided to deal with Hannibal. Don't ask me why I decided to become a black militant in a North Korean prison camp in 1952. I had always admired Hannibal and his military exploits. I admired him even more because he had black skin. If I had been as smart as I thought I was, I would have talked about Confucious or some of those other Asians. But, no, not this James Thompson. I wanted to talk about my Hannibal. I did. As a consequence, my cherished Hannibal almost got me killed.

During my presentation about Hannibal, I went overboard, telling how this great black general kicked the Romans' ass all over the place and did masterful things with his elephants during a trek across the snow-covered Alps.

I guess, looking back, I was subconsciously trying to establish the superiority of a great black general.

"Tell me, comrade," Chop Suey interrupted, when did Rome kick Hannibal's ass?"

He was cute. The little screwball was cute. I didn't have to be brilliant to realize Chop Suey was ticked off. I had gotten to him and he was fuming. The problem now was preventing him from getting to me.

"Well," I recalled fumbling, "Hannibal ran into a few problems with his allies. Some of his friends in Italy, Macedonia, Syracuse and Sicily became too preoccupied with their own interests to maintain the heavy support they had given him earlier . . ."

"Don't want excuse!" Chop Suey shouted. "I only want to know when they kicked your man Hannibal's ass. That's all! When did they get his butt?"

Chop Suey was losing his cool a bit. I had to take care he didn't become irresponsible. Protecting Hannibal's image was one thing. Protecting my ass was something else.

"The Roman general Scipio finally defeated this great warrior at Zama, in Northern Africa, around 202 B.C. But, they didn't kill him! He eventually committed suicide years later rather than be taken prisoner by the Romans."

Chop Suey just stared at me rather expressionless, sort of picking his teeth. I could see members of my group, especially Willie, looking at him carefully, trying to survey his mood in an effort to anticipate the bastard's actions.

"You very smart man, aren't you comrade?" Chop Suey was now on a fishing expedition. I really had to be careful now. Couldn't let my answers have a bearing on my butt. These little screwballs were devious and dangerous. To be sure, they were

# True Colors

always polite. I remember seeing a guard "politely" invite a POW out of formation one day and beat the hell out of him. Then he politely helped the fallen POW up and, with the utmost of courtesy, politely escorted the bloodied soldier back into formation.

"Well, I try to keep abreast of things," I answered, trying my best to sound matter of factly and doing a poor job of it.

"I see," he quietly responded. "I see. Comrade why don't you come with me. I won't take too long."

The die was cast! I had gambled that I could get away with being a smart ass and had apparently lost. I girded myself for some type of punishment. I had also resolved to die fighting back if the punishment became too uncivil. For one, I wasn't going to let them stick a goddamn water hose down my throat . . . not while I was alive. I would take a beating, perhaps become a bit bloodied, but I wouldn't just stand there like a pig and let anyone pull my fingernails out without a fight. Bravery and courage had nothing to do with it. I just hate to be subjected to uncivilized pain. Sticking a water hose down my mouth and cutting the water on is what I call uncivilized pain.

I was led to a shack and told to stand in the center of the room until someone came for me. Except for a desk and chair and a small mirror on the wall, the room was virtually empty. I stood there for about an hour before realizing that this was perhaps going to be my punishment. Hell! If this was going to be all, I had it made. I could stand in the middle of a goddamn room forever, just as long as someone brought me a little food and water. I recall actually feeling a bit smug and comfortable . . . and victorious! I had outsmarted them and was even getting away with light punishment. Damn! I felt smug! In fact, I began to feel a bit macho. Screw the little asses! Someone once said that "each victory tends to make one stronger." Whoever said it never lied. At that very moment I felt like a giant! I remember feeling that way after I had stood up to a white police officer during my early years in Arkansas. He shouted at me and I shouted back. I wasn't being brave. I was just angry and didn't take time to think about the possible consequences. Later, when I did think about it, I almost became ill from fear of what could have happened because I wasn't more than twelve years old at the time.

After about an hour and a half, Chop Suey returned with "Bop Daddy". Mr. Dapper himself. He also returned with Kim-Sing, my old comrade from my days on the ice. I knew right away this was not an assemblage of goodwill. I was particularly wary of Kim-Sing. WE just didn't have any good blood at all for each other.

I should have suspected "Bop Daddy" figured somewhere in the picture the minute I saw the mirror on the wall. True to form, he entered the room and walked nonchalantly over to the mirror, briefly brushing his hair.

"Good to see you again, Comrade Thompson. Glad to see you doing so well in class."

These little midgets were forever playing games.

"Thank you, sir," I acknowledged stiffly.

I was braced and I think "Bop Daddy" knew it.

"Relax, comrade, relax. We your friends. My comrade here tells me I should marvel at how much you know. I just wanted to find out for myself. Great minds are to be respected. Don't you agree?"

As I have said repeatedly, I have always resented people who patronized me. It was the worst form of condescension. I had experienced well meaning whites doing it to me in Arkansas. Now, I was having it done to me by a jive talking Communist Chinese in North Korea.

"I understand, comrade, you know ALL about Hannibal and the Romans. How Hannibal kicked their rumps all over the place."

He was becoming quite sarcastic. As wary as I was of him, I kept my eyes focused on Kim-Sing. He kept watching me with a scowl as he stood there with his arms folded. I knew full well that if he were unleashed on me, I was in for a long evening. We had gone into the shack about three-thirty in the afternoon.

"I have always taken a liking to history," I replied calmly, trying to plot my next move in this verbal chess game.

"Good! Good, comrade! Let's talk about China. Tell me what you know about our homeland, China."

"Bop Daddy" sat down and for the first time really looked at me. The pressure was now on. We had been told quite a bit about China and the role Communism played there. I tried to quickly recall some of the things I had read in school years earlier. If I could recall anything, this was now the place and time to start recalling.

"Well," I began slowly, "the capital of China is Peking . . ."

"Everybody knows that, comrade." "Bop Daddy" interrupted, "tell me other things."

I wanted to say the nation has been ripped repeatedly by famine, that most of the people were poor as hell and dying of starvation. But I didn't and I knew darn well I wouldn't.

"Well, China is the third largest country in the world. It reportedly has more people . . ."

"Reportedly?" shot back Chop Suey. "I never told you it 'reportedly' has more people."

"Either it has more people or it doesn't," "Bop Daddy" stated rather calmly in that disinterested voice of his. This man just gave the impression of being above all this.

"Okay," I began to correct, "China has more people than any other nation. About a fifth of all the people in the world live in China . . ."

"Uh huh, very good, comrade," "Bop Daddy" remarked as he stood and walked over by the mirror, starting to brush his locks again. I never considered him a faggot. Just a man who was chronically vain.

"What type government runs China?" "Bop Daddy" asked, never turning from the mirror.

"It has a Communist dictatorship," I fired back, not once realizing what I had actually said.

"It has a what?" jumped in Chop Suey.

"A dictatorship?" quipped "Bop Daddy," turning now from the mirror and walking over close to me.

"I mean simply that there are no problem with political infighting . . . everybody understands what's expected and does it."

I knew I had put my foot into it and wasn't even coming close to taking it out. At this point I am not sure they were even listening. The scowl on Kim-Sing's face was wider than ever. He was just aching to get at me and I seemed to have been trying to hasten that possibility. I had to be more careful about things that were very sensitive to these bastards, even if it was the truth.

"No dictatorship! Understand? No dictatorship!" "Bop Daddy" had never demonstrated so much energy. He proved to be a little rooster after all.

"The Chinese people are proud people," he continued. "We take pride in our country, our achievements. Our history is rich in culture! Our influence on other nations strong. Strong! Hear me, comrade? Strong! Other nations, they borrow from our technology, our art, our language, our philosophy. No goddamn dictatorship! That's imperialistic propaganda and you know it!"

At that he walked over to the mirror, brushed his hair, gave me a blistering glare and stalked out of the room.

"Be back! You stay! I be back!"

He slammed the door! Chop Suey and Kim-Sing whispered a few words to each other, then Chop Suey left. Back to the pits was my first reaction. I had been thrown to the lions again.

Kim-Sing only had a pistol on him, no baseball bats or rifle butts. At least I was thankful for that. This man hated my guts.

"You wanna apologize for that wisecrack 'bout our government?" Kim-Sing asked while taking his pistol out and holding it at "parade rest."

One has to appreciate for one's self the real anxiety that comes from having another son-of-a-bitch point a gun at you. This is more so when the person pointing the gun is angry. Add to, this no knowledge whatsoever of what's going through the gun-

# True Colors

pointer's mind. If you knew for sure he was bluffing, that's one thing. But, if you don't know this you just sort of go into a stupor of fear, nothing actually seeming real.

"Well, I didn't intend to be insulting," I said in response to the bastard's request.

"That ain't no apology!" he shouted, slapping the shit out of me. He really teed me off. Talking about seeing stars and red. He caught me totally unprepared for the blow. That wallop brought tears to my eyes. I thought for a moment he was going to hit me with that pistol too. He momentarily hoisted the gun as if to strike, but he didn't. Damn! That lick hurt!

"Okay, okay, I apologize," I added quickly.

"You black monkeys only understand violence. I stop talk to you. I beat you butt. You appreciate that! White man deal with you by beatin' your butts. I beat some butts over here too. You black asses too stubborn. Too stubborn! You black asses too stubborn. Too stubborn! Now tell me 'bout China and tell me somethin' good. Speak up!" He again raised his hand as if to pop me but I pulled away.

"Well, I was once told that China has seven of the world's largest fifty cities. That Chinese history goes back more than three thousand years . . . that Chinese scholars are generally well respected . . . that the Chinese were the first to develop things like the compass, paper, gunpowder and printing. That agriculture is the main thing."

How I wanted to add that China can barely produce enough food to feed its people. Again, wishful thinking. Such an innocent statement of fact could have easily cost me my life, such as it was.

"I remember you ass from the ice detail. You were smart ass then and you are smart ass now. You what the whites call one of them uppity niggers.

"You went so far as to piss on my ice! Even when I told you don't do it, you still went on pissing!"

Again, he slammed his hand into my unsuspecting face. I

felt the trickle of warm blood through the nose.

"You smart nigger! Smart nigger! Go 'head, piss on my floor! You pissed on my ice. Do it on the floor! Do it and I blow your uppity head off . . . knock it right in the middle of your stinkin' piss. You bum! Black bum!"

He was really baiting the hell out of me. Quite frankly, I didn't at that point know how many more blows I would take before he would have to use that pistol. Life without personal dignity isn't worth living. My clock of patience was now clicking down. Nothing was funny anymore.

Again he ripped me across the face. I bent down for a few moments, trying to decide whether to strike then or after the next blow. If I wanted to end it all right then and there. If I wanted to go for a kill on this bastard and be executed later in the afternoon, as surely I would be.

"Git ovah there!"

He caught me by my torn shirt collar and rammed me into the table, knocking the shit out of my forehead. I felt a small gash on my forehead, blood now dripping on my shirt . . . and the floor.

"Don't drip cheap black blood on that clean floor! Take off shirt! Take off shirt! Quick nigger or you die right now! Take it off in a hurry!"

I quickly complied.

"Now wipe up that cheap blood! Wipe it all up. Who give you right to drip blood on the people's floor!"

This little son-of-a-bitch was really pressing our luck. I knew that when I nailed him I had just as soon kill him. I would certainly be put to death so there would be little reason to take it easy on his ass.

I busied myself wiping the few blood droppings from the floor.

"You people ain't good enough men to drop blood on our floors. You don't drop them on white people floors back home do you? And you ain't gonna drop them on our floors here. Wipe!

Wipe!"

I hadn't been wiping for more than about thirty seconds when I felt this warm liquid pouring over my hands. I looked up quickly to see this rotten son-of-a-bitch urinating over my hands and shirt. He backed away a few feet then stopped.

"Look down in front of you, nigger! Look good 'cause one more step and that's where you die!"

He cocked his pistol, pulling the hammer back and locking it. Although I was fully prepared to die, I had no intention of attempting suicide alone. If I went, he went with me.

From my distance I had no chance of getting him before he got off enough rounds to stop me in my tracks.

"C'mon, your move! C'mon! You seem to be tired of living!"

He had the upper hand and we both knew it. I remember just standing and staring at the little sucker. He stood smiling and waving the pistol playfully in the air in front of me. All I needed was about four feet closer to him and neither of us, no doubt, would ever see a tomorrow.

The impasse was broken by the sound of someone coming. Kim-Sing quickly put away his pistol and opened the door. "Bop Daddy" and Chop Suey had returned.

"What happened to him?" Bop Daddy asked Kim-Sing, noticing the blood on my forehead.

"Oh, he stumbled, hit head on table," the idiot lied.

"See to it, comrade," "Bop Daddy" tried to advise, "that you remember less about Hannibal and more about Chairman Mao. He is the answer to the problems of the poor Third World peoples. Your own Abe Lincoln said 'All men are created equal'. Chairman Mao is just trying to ensure that all men are given an equal chance at being happy. Why fight what makes so much sense, huh? Why fight what makes so much sense?"

Why indeed. Kim-Sing had just slapped me repeatedly. He had just rammed me into a damn desk, ripping the hell out of my forehead. He had pissed all over my hands, had me wipe up my own blood while it was being diluted by his own piss. I had been threatened at gunpoint and cursed out. Why, indeed, fight what makes so much damn sense?"

## Burial Rituals Challenged

The Chinese were very suspicious and downright bitter toward any secret organization such as the Masons. This was dramatically called to our attention shortly after the death of Mack Parker, one of our Masonic brothers. Although this will never be proved, we suspect that Mack died of malnutrition.

When it came time to bury him, those of us who were Masons volunteered for the burial detail. The guard assigned to accompany us was a quiet little fellow we called "Italy."

He was a nice enough chap, I guess. Just didn't say too much. He would just look at you with a faint smile. These people did believe in smiling.

We pitched in digging Mack's grave and, just before lowering the body, commenced to go through a bit of Masonic gravesite ritual. At the time none of us paid much attention to "Italy." We knew he was standing there observing us, but we simply didn't direct much attention to him. Mack's burial was about as solemn as burials are. He was really a nice guy. Quiet fellow.

That same afternoon, although he didn't participate, but because he was the camp POW representative, Sergeant Freddie was called in and dressed down about the burial. "Bop Daddy" demanded that he interpret every word and sign used during the Masonic gravesite ritual for Mack. "Italy" had reported us, apparently explaining that we were using signs and words in codes.

"No more secret talk and signs at burials." "Bop Daddy" warned "No more! We find that what you tell me is lie, you be punished!"

"Punished severely! Just bury comrade and leave. Pray okay. But no secret talk. Understand?"

I must explain that we lied like dogs about the nature of our rituals. As any loyal Mason knows, secrecy among the brotherhood is part of its strength, the common bond that binds. Since we all knew that "Bop Daddy" could not determine the accuracy of our statements about ritual, we sort of made up the explanation as we went along. Since there were no repercussions later, we had apparently been successful with our deception.

Another incident about burials comes to mind. Since most of the blacks in the compound were Baptists steeped in the heavy Baptist tradition, we customarily bowed our heads while one of us took the lead in saying a rather emotional prayer, as any God-fearing Baptist usually does. I remember going to Baptist churches where the prayers were longer and more emotional than the sermons. You were graded by your ability to pray. Either you were a "good prayer" or a "bad prayer." No in between. When you get down on your knees in a black Baptist church, there can be no slow stepping. As my mother would always say, "You gotta strut your stuff for the Master."

At any rate, word got back to us that "Italy" had accompanied a group of white POWs on a burial detail and noticed that they failed to bow their heads on one occasion. According to the report, "Italy" became quite upset and made them bow their heads at gunpoint.

One thing I must say, funerals are big things with blacks, especially those in the rural South. Usually when a black person dies in the rural South, his station in life is determined by how many people show up at the funeral and how emotional the services. A poor turnout and a lackluster service was interpreted as "not being well thought of at all." But, a huge turnout and services that had people falling in the aisles with emotion would usually be interpreted as a "great funeral," amid cries of "a community giant has gone home." So, the idea was to line up as many friends as possible during life so that when you left this place someone got the notion that you had made some great contribution to living. Didn't matter that you were a weasel and a cheat. The point was everybody knew you. It could not be said that you were just an everyday ordinary weasel and cheat. You were exceptional. Then, too, no one said anything bad at funerals. You could always count on that. The ministers would always manage to say the right things. Even arch enemies seem to come around. It's amazing, those rural Southern Baptist funerals.

# 10
# Lice Plague

Lice! This became a major camp problem. Those little things were everywhere. They were in the lining of our jackets, in our pant seams, forever crawling on our bodies. The little creatures seemed to especially delight in attacking our heads. I remember quite vividly how we would take turns cracking them from our bodies. Some of us tried putting our jackets out in the cold weather in hope of killing the dreaded lice. But, this was all to no avail. When we brought our clothes back in the heat from our bodies would hatch the eggs and the agony would begin once more. It was a bitch! Crack! Crack! Crack! They were everywhere! The sight of men cracking lice was almost continuous.

Poppa Browne eventually came up with one of those down home remedies for getting rid of the lice, at least it eased the problem somewhat. He made us cut a large drum in half, something to use as a large tub. We then put the water-filled drum on the fire, bringing it to a boil. Poppa Browne then told to put ashes from the fire in the boiling water. Then, he told us to place as many of our clothes as possible in that ash-filled water. As the steaming water lashed into those clothes we looked to see if we could actually see the little monsters leaping their butts off our clothing. "I coulda told y'all two months ago that boilin' water was the onliest way to kill lice," Willie Fields remarked once as we watched the boiling water. "I didn't say nuttin' 'cause I knew none of y'all would believe me. So, I jes let 'em eat y'all ass. I can't tell ya nuttin'. Won't either."

"Willie," Sgt. Josh Logan quipped, "how would ya like to take a dip in there with 'em lice, huh?"

"Why don't we both take a dip in thar? I keep tellin' ya blood, ya simply ain't got 'nuff ass to come afta mine. No way!"

"C'mon, guys, knock it off," Poppa Browne's voice of quiet authority would be respected, even by Willie, unless it was a point of debate.

I must point out here that even though the boiling did ease the problem somewhat, we were never really freed of the lice dilemma. Our compound was too infested. We would have had to throw every stitch of clothing as well as our bodies in that drum to have eliminated the problem, not that the thought was completely foreign to us. We became quite desperate at times.

### Physical Condition

Prior to my imprisonment I was a solid 185 pounds. When I weighed myself in mid-1951 I was down to 97 pounds. I had become a mere skeleton of a man, with outlines of ribs plainly visible. Our overall body resistance was extremely low, making us quite susceptible to all types of diseases.

At one point, the entire camp suffered an outbreak of a dreaded seven-day flu. We called it the "seven-day flu" because some of the more serious cases usually died within five days. Everyone became quite concerned about it.

I managed to survive the first rash of flu outbreaks, finally coming down with it just as the outbreak was beginning to ease. I was taken to the hospital and placed with other POWs suffering with the flu. I do recall that first night, the grunts and groans all over the place.

At one point during my stay in the hospital, I remember the guard shouting "halt" at me while I stood in the doorway. I must have been delirious because for the life of me I don't remember getting off the floor. I only remember standing there listening to some guard shout "halt." I didn't stop. I merely walked sluggishly back to my quarters. I was pretty much out of it and simply didn't give a damn whether they shot me or not at that particular point. I was defiant. When pain craves relief, common sense sits in the back seat.

Poppa Browne and several others, including Willie, begged me to lie down. I recall hearing someone say, "Tom will never make it." Even amid the throes of death, the struggle for survival is intense. Man's basic instinct is to survive. Even if he knows full well that death is inevitable, he will still try to defy those odds in a last-ditch effort at survival. I recall reading accounts of the Jews in Poland's Warsaw ghetto during World War Two and their almost fanatical fight against an overwhelming Nazi force. I recall admiring how they fought zealously with bricks, bottles, and a few guns against tanks and mortars. There was simply no way they could win . . . but they fought for weeks against those incredible odds. They were simply trying to survive in the face of almost certain death.

As long as man's mind is free, he will fight and fight to the death if need be. He will never submit to death without a struggle, as long as his mind is free. He will resign to punishment, even slavery, as long as the opportunity to live is there. But, threaten death, and even slaves will rebel. It's the natural law of survival. In order to strike back during captivity, one must first fight to protect the mind. This is everything! Once the mind goes, then, eventually, the body becomes a robot, available to every whim of a captor.

Sure, my fever was a bitch! But, I wasn't mentally resigned to death. Whenever I leave this world, I plan to do so fighting for one more breath. Then, too, I had added motivation for wanting to survive in North Korea. I wanted to tell this story. If no one except my immediate family ever read it, fine! At least I will be freed of the mental need to tell somebody that we, as blacks, didn't have a free ride while captives of the Communists in North Korea. All that hogwash about one minority treating another minority with respect is a bunch of Mississippi bullshit! There are too many black graves all over North and South Korea offering grim testimony to the contrary. During World War Two the Japanese soldiers didn't exactly offer black American soldiers tea when they met on the battlefields in the Pacific. Each was trying desperately to blow each other's guts out and usually did. Japanese and black soldiers on the battlefields didn't lay their weapons down, run and embrace each other, and begin discussing the solidarity of Third World Peoples. When those little suckers came running through those jungles shouting "Banzai" they were after my ass, black or white, that wore an American uniform. That Third World stuff is fine for radicals preaching on the streets of New York, but on the battlefields it isn't worth a good damn. Anyone who has ever witnessed a group of Communist Chinese running fanatically down a slope in Korea knows all too well they aren't making color distinctions.

What's more, I don't recall any black American soldiers standing up in their foxholes waving "C'mon brothers" to the little midgets as they came down those slopes. It was ass kicking time, not an ethnic reunion.

Two days after returning from the hospital my fever broke. Thanks to the two G.I., P.O.W. doctors who ate with the Chinese, stole two aspirin and dropped them along the fence line, I am alive today. Strangely, to my knowledge, these U.S. officers were never accused of collaborating. People can put down aspirins if they want to, but I credit two of the little things with saving my life. I survived through the seventh day, a day I was expected to die if the trend for fever victims continued. In fact, I survived with a healthier than usual appetite. I can remember aggressively eating all of the lousy stuff they gave us. I was feeling better, actually better than I had felt in months. I recall still another time when I suffered with a bad toothache. There was no real dentist in the camp, so I went to a guy who was acting as a dentist, and asked him to help me. He put my head in the window and using a pair of pliers he proceeded to pull my tooth. There was no anesthesia, no pain killer of any kind. Pain was like torture. He tugged and tugged until the tooth cracked loose with an even more terrifying sharp pain. After that ordeal and recovery I didn't ever have another tooth extracted. I remember my rapid recovery sparked many jokes.

"With the appetite ya got now," Willie snapped, "it wuz better for our stomachs if ya had just gone on and died."

"Thompson," even Poppa Browne joined in, 'next time you git that close to dyin' we're gonna give death equal time."

Despite the jokes, I was alive and well. Old Thompson was still here. And eating more, if not better.

After that episode, I learned a valuable lesson. Never drink any more water unless I boiled it. Normally, I would do this, putting the water in a canteen I kept around me most of the time. But, from time to time, depending on the weather, I would run out of canteen water and be tempted to drink from a pump. I knew better, but I would drink from it occasionally anyway. But, no more. I had witnessed a fellow POW drink from it and double over several minutes later. Since it was warm that day, I related this POW's death to the heat and overall malnutrition, never the unsanitary pump. But, no more chances. Boiled water from that point on.

Boiled water had other advantages. It kept us from getting worms. Most of the POWs suffered from severe worm problems. Sometimes when I would lie still, I could just feel the sensation of worms inside me. It was weird. Between the lice, the fever and the worms, we seemed at times to be waging a losing battle. But, there was no choice. We had to find the strength to keep going. As Poppa Browne would keep urging, "What's the use giving up here? We will always have to fight. Stateside we will still have to fight racism. Here, we're fighting brutality and starvation. A fight's a fight! One fight keeps you in shape for the other. So, fellows, let's stay in shape. Let's all resolve to never break training!" That became my own little rallying cry, "never break training," never give up.

Although most of us had been doing a minimum of daily exercise, we decided to increase our regimen just a bit in order to retain not only physical fitness but mental toughness. One cannot be soft and survive in hostile and hard surroundings. Make no mistake, it is not easy doing exercise when the body is weak. One tends to crave sleep and rest. But, we all knew that to do the exercises in our physical state would be to also challenge and harden our mental state.

"Hut, Two, three, four. Hut, two, three four."

We all took turns leading the daily exercise regimen. I can recall quite well the day Willie led us through our paces.

"One, two, three, four. C'mon, girls, let's git to it! Y'all bendin' ovah like ya wuz a bunch of bitches. C'mon! One, two, three, four. Hit it! One, two, three, four! Talkin' 'bout being men. Shit! Y'all's a bunch of girls. Sissies! C'mon Logan! You da main one. Talkin' 'bout gittin 'n my ass. Shucks! Cain't even bend ovah. Hit it! One, two, three, four. One, two, three, four . . ."

One thing about Willie, for a man in captivity, he had one of the most gung-ho dispositions. Willie didn't need to develop any more mental toughness. He was so ornery until mental toughness was built in. As long as Willie had some kind of edge on the rest of us, he had some vehicle on which to feed. Mind you, Willie was not malicious. Far from it. He was just basically cantankerous. I had a relative like Willie. If you told him the sun was hot, he might say "don't jump to unproven conclusions." This world just had too many imperfections in it for Willie. If he had his way, I do believe Willie would have destroyed this present life and re-made the whole damn universe. Willie's way.

"C'mon, git off yo' ass, girls and swing 'em arms. Swing 'em!

Way back! Thatta way! Thatta way! Thatta way girls. One, two, three, four. One, two, three, four. C'mon. Hit it! No wondah we'se losing the war. Nuttin' but a buncha damn sissies on our side. Where'd they git y'all from anyway? C'mon! Bend 'em backs! If I had y'all back home for 'bout two weeks in dem cotton fields I'd make men outta ya. Hit it!"

Willie was in his glory. Perspiration completely saturating his body, he kept at it, seeming to love the torture he was administering. He knew many of us couldn't take it. He knew exactly what he was doing. He was gaining bragging rights for the rest of the day.

"Don't over do it, Willie," came a bit of advice from an exhausted Poppa Browne. "The idea is to keep us in shape. Not help the enemy kill us. Don't over do it now."

I ain't ovah doin' nuttin, "y'all jes can't take it that's all. Y'all jes soft. Y'all shudda stayed home and helped ya maw with her sewin'. Hit it! One, two, three, four. One, two, three, four. If ya call yo'self a man then be a man. Do it! Sway yo' bodies! Sway 'em hard! Like this! Like this! One, two, three, four. One, two, three, four . . ."

Willie was making his goddamn point. When he conducted our exercises, he always did. He wanted and he would have his bragging rights. One thing about Willie no one ever doubted. He was indeed a man. A braggart, yes. Cantankerous, yes. Grumpy, yes. A weakling, no way!

# 11
# Escape Fizzled

I recall that several of us were being taken on a work detail in a rather wooded area. Looking back, I don't remember what kind of work we were supposed to be doing out there. It appeared, at least to me, that we were forever being taken on work details. Some of it didn't make any sense. But, you can bet the Chinese had a purpose. Everything they did was by design.

It was fairly early in the morning. The little guard accompanying us apparently hadn't gotten much sleep the night before because he appeared half awake as he led us wearily through the woods alongside a steep hill. Looked to me as if his eyes were closed. Once or twice he nearly tripped and fell, bringing muffled laughter from some of us.

"No talk! No talk! he demanded, continuing his trance-like pace. The bastard was grumpy as all hell. If this guard could have just blown our asses over the hill and gone back to sleep I got the impression the world would have been just fine to him. He was out of it. But, he had that machine gun dangling from his shoulders.

We had walked for about forty-five minutes before our little

# True Colors

sleepy guard told us to take a break. None of us had the faintest notion where we were going. In fact, some of us doubted if our sleepy friend even knew or cared. There were seven of us. We sat down in a semi-circle, with the guard sitting in front of us, his back resting on a tree. I noticed that the bastard was getting too goddamn comfortable. After a fashion, he began to nod his head slowly, then abruptly catch himself before falling off into a deep sleep entirely. He did this several times before I began to really toy with a possibility. Escape! Chances were I would never get a better opportunity.

At one point I signalled to the G.I. next to me that the guard was rapidly falling asleep and that we could at least attempt to make a break for it.

"You'd never make it across those lines," I recall him whispering back to me. "They'd have your ass 'fore night."

"Gotta try. We should at least try," I remember saying.

"I agree," he shot back. I just don't think the time is right. Not just yet. That sucker is liable to kill somebody this morning. We gotta be careful. I think I will wait awhile."

I could well understand my fellow G.I.'s caution. An irritable, sleepy and armed guard is dangerous. Anyone in his right mind knows this to be a given truth. You don't go tempting an armed guard who is rest broken. Nothing is funny or playful about this type creature. I knew it and my friend knew it.

I decided to wait too. I just sat and watched the little son-of-a-bitch. He wasn't more than five feet four. We could easily overpower his little rump, take that machine gun and haul-ass out of there. Great idea. But who in the hell was going to try for the machine gun? You don't pounce on a half sleepy armed guard. If he awakened abruptly he could shoot the shit out of all of us. The thing to do was let this sleeping dog lie. He was simply too dangerous. Then, too, I think there was something about the way he was holding that weapon. It was resting on his lap with a finger on the trigger. He could begin spraying us in less than a second. That was too quick! Even superman couldn't move on him that fast.

I kept watching him. The G.I. next to me was watching him too. We were both playing chess games. Do we move now or wait? Could we make it back to our lines? Where in the hell were our lines? Had we launched a new offensive? Were we still being pushed back? Too many questions and too few answers. Seemed safer just to stay put.

Right or wrong, I decided to try it. My friend next to me gave the old "thumbs up" good luck sign. I wondered briefly why he didn't join me. I also wondered briefly why I didn't just let well enough alone and stay with him. But, I was mentally committed. I wanted out!

I slowly rolled away from the group, moving inches at a time. The other POWs, bless their everlasting hearts, moved their bodies out of my way in an effort to give me clear sailing. They then resumed their positions in an attempt to conceal my exit. Comradeship during war can be a beautiful thing: a symphony when it's working. On this particular morning the symphony was playing beautifully.

I had to be careful not to break a twig or do anything that might snap our sleepy friend out of it. This could be dangerous not only for myself but to my fellow POWs as well.

I kept rolling. Six feet. Eight feet. Twelve. Twenty-five. I wanted to thank Willie for his rigorous training sessions. They were paying off after all. They were taking my black butt out of North Korea. Sorry, I couldn't say goodbye to the gang, but I was sure they would understand. They would even applaud my courage. My deed might even instill a special defiance throughout the entire compound. I was beginning to feel good. I didn't bother to pause for rest. Had to roll far enough away from the group before I stood and put my long, lanky though weak legs to good use. I knew I could run. Rolling was something else. I rolled about sixty feet before standing up. I didn't start to run immediately. Still didn't want to make any noise. I must have tiptoed another sixty or seventy feet before I started to run. Haul ass was more like it. 'I came to a small hill, climbed it and began making my way down the other side. I tripped in my haste and tumbled seemingly forever before slamming into the ground below. Dammit! That hurt! In North Korea even the small hills are deceptively steep. I noticed blood on my forehead. I wiped it on my sleeves and kept dashing along the side of the hill. I really didn't give a good damn how far our lines were, I was on my way.

Make no mistake, I was not trotting. I was running! I was free! I didn't want any son-of-a-bitch stopping me now. Old James Thompson was rounding third and heading home. I thought about Poppa Browne, Logan, Willie and the entire gang. How I would miss their marvelous butts. But, I had a chance for freedom and I was taking it. I was thinking all of these wonderful thoughts when suddenly I smelled what appeared to be parched corn. I thought it must have been a little village on the other side of the little hill directly in front of me. I slowly began climbing that little obstacle and got almost halfway up before I heard what sounded like people talking. I really became worried because the words appeared to be Chinese. I was now on my belly, not knowing what to expect when I got to the top of the hill.

By now my body was a dish rag. Sweat dripped from head to toe. Nervous tension was now taking its toll. My joy was slowly turning to panic. Who in the hell were they? A patrol? Who?

When I got to the top of the hill and looked over I was shocked! Stunned! About fifty yards from me two Chinese guards with fixed bayonets were slapping a white POW around. The poor guy had both hands tied over his head. He was a bloody mess. One guard kicked him in the stomach, tumbling the G.I. to the ground. They quickly grabbed him, stood the poor fellow up and kicked him again. He cried out in agony.

Another shock! Beyond the trio I noticed what appeared to be the other side of our prison compound! The white side! In my haste I had apparently run to the outer extremity of the white POW compound. In running around those winding hills I had inadvertently come full circle. I was now behind the white POW compound, although several hundred yards on the outside of it. My sense of direction had been piss poor! But I was still out. Still free! Had to haul ass out of there and reverse my direction.

Good idea but too late. One of the guards with the white POW saw me. He wasted little time shouting at me and firing in my direction. To say I moved out fast is an understatement. This tall, lanky, Arkansas farm boy moved! At one point I slammed head-on into a small tree. That son-of-a-bitch came out of nowhere! One minute it wasn't there; the next minute I was right in the middle of it. Damn that hurt!

Another shot from behind me! That bastard was now chasing me! Two more shots! I didn't think I could run any faster but I sincerely believe I did. Fatigue was not a factor. It never is when death is chasing your rump.

I must say this, however, I was getting pretty goddamn tired of running from these little midgets. It seemed as if the better part of my life in North Korea was spent on the run from little people behind me with a gun.

I tried to run and think at the same time. I remembered the sleepy guard. I don't think he had even the remotest idea how many of us he was supposed to be guarding. He was too out of it. That being true, if I made it back to my compound I could lose myself since I was too far away from the guard chasing me to have been recognized. Trying to continue my escape now was silly. I would never make it. Didn't have the strength. It was now ass saving time. If I were lucky, I would see Poppa Browne Willie, Logan and the entire gang again afterall. If I were lucky! There was still this little runt breathing down my rear with that rifle.

Thanks to pure panic I finally made it back to my side of the camp compound. I stopped long enough to pick up some wood, giving the impression I was just returning from a detail. Another damn good job of acting was very much needed . . . and right then!

I got back to my quarters exhausted. Poppa Browne and two

others were mopping and dusting. I flopped down on the floor, too tired to explain my recent ordeal. Almost instantly the door opened and the guard entered, with an interpreter. He looked around the room, surveying each of us carefully. It didn't take a genius to determine the most likely suspect. I was wet all over, looking exhausted, with blood pouring down my forehead.

"You!" the interpreter began, pointing at me, "you on other side of compound? Outside? Answer up!"

I was exhausted. Too exhausted to stand.

"Yes," I responded wearily. "Yes, it was me."

"He just returned from a wood detail," Poppa Browne intervened. "Anything wrong?"

Ignoring Poppa Browne's question, the two guards spoke in Chinese for a few moments. Then the interpreter requested that I follow them to headquarters.

"Shit!" I remember saying quietly. I had run my butt half way across North Korea, or at least it seemed, only to end up going to headquarters.

"Damn shame," I thought. "Damn shame."

Prior to leaving, the interpreter spoke to Poppa Browne, telling him that I would not be long. I could sense some type of disagreement between the interpreter and the guard. I surmised it was over whether or not I should be taken, whether it was I who was spying on their little atrocity. At any rate, I was taken to headquarters.

When we arrived at headquarters, I was told to wait outside. It was about three o'clock then. When they finally made up their little minds to call me in, it was pretty close to seven o'clock. They were artists at having us wait. I suspected they did this to unnerve us, to make it easier to crack us mentally.

I had expected to see "Bop Daddy". However, I was greeted by another officer. A stern looking bastard. He wasn't any cutie pie. All business. No nonsense.

The interpreter began by asking what I was doing on the other side of the compound. I responded that I was on a wood detail.

"Why you come back way you did? By white compound?" the officer asked through the interpreter.

I had to think of a convincing lie. Witnessing what you aren't supposed to witness is dangerous at any time, during war or peace. It was more so for an American in captivity in North Korea in 1952. What's more, I was that unlucky American.

"That was my first time working that area," I began to lie, "so I really wasn't too familiar. The group I was with left me to finish up the spot I was working in. When I finished I decided to try and take a short cut back. I got confused and a bit lost."

I didn't have time to evaluate how convincing it sounded. At least I had said something. I didn't just stand there like a babbling idiot.

"Were you trying to escape, comrade?"

This sucker didn't waste time coming to the point. I had to be extremely careful, and wide awake. If I fell mentally asleep, I'd find myself on my ass and I knew it.

"No, comrade. Escape never occurred to me. I wouldn't know where to go."

At least I was half right. I was trying to escape but it was now apparent to me I didn't know where the hell it was I was going.

"Comrade, did you see anything unusual when you come down hill?"

"Uh, I don't know what you mean, sir."

I was trying to buy some time, gather my thoughts. While I was trying to gather whatever it was I wanted to gather, the officer struck me across the face, blood gushing from my mouth. I had encountered another son-of-a-bitch who could hit. That bastard was quick too. I didn't even see that slap coming. I've never fully understood why these people didn't hold more world boxing titles. Some of them hit like hell, quick as cats!

When the officer slapped me, the interpreter even looked astonished. The officer said something in Chinese, then turned and abruptly walked from the room. I've never been more glad to see a man leave my presence. The sting on my face lingered long after he had left.

The interpreter then took over, telling me I must answer all questions and to stop being a cutie pie. He warned that there was nothing but pain associated with being a cutie pie. I was the first to agree. The interpreter at least appeared to be humane. He was a scholarly type, probably a college professor. I began to relax, realizing he was no threat to me physically.

My mental comfort was short lived, however, because in about ten minutes the officer returned, his face more stern than ever. I surmised that "the professor" was a part of the act, softening me for the second round. As I've said countless times, everything the Chinese did, seemed to have some design attached to it.

"Why did you come five thousand miles to fight Koreans?" the officer resumed, not a hint of humanity on his face.

"Because my government sent me," was my tense response, surprising even me.

"Did you know your government was wrong, dead wrong?"

"No!" I shot back, deciding to keep my answers short and sweet, all the time keeping my eyes on that right hand of his.

"Well, I tell you they wrong," he began to lecture, "wrong to come over here to fight innocent Koreans. Wrong come here to spy on Chinese people. We warn your government. But no listen! Hard head your government. Hard head. As for you . . ."

I remember him walking around me a bit, surveying me suspiciously.

"As for you, you disgrace to your own people. To all Third World people. You let yourself be used by a government that does not recognize you as human being. You fool."

The old racial tactic again. They would use this many times during our captivity. Poppa Browne had warned us over and over about the enemy's artful use of this ploy. Regardless, it still made your blood boil, especially when you couldn't respond to this bullshit.

I can still see myself standing there boiling, my mouth cut inside and bleeding from that blow. Although, I never refused to answer his questions, he still had to show me he was in authority. I guess this was one of those times that I began to think quite hard and heavy about home. I certainly thought about Florence. . . about more tranquil times. I had to keep control over both my mind and my anger.

"I sick of you!" the officer finally shouted, ending the session. "Get this pig outta my sight before I throw up! Get him OUTTA HERE!"

The interpreter quickly hustled me out of the room. If the outburst was meant to demean me, it was effective. I must admit to feeling quite low. I was a grown man who didn't particularly like being shouted at by anyone. But to be shouted at in a condescending manner was too much. To accept this without retaliation was even more agonizing. Captivity is no place for a proud man. There is too much crow you have to eat, especially if survival means anything.

# 12
# More Dashed Hopes

Things took an incredible turn for the best around the first of March 1953. None of us related it to anything in particular at first. At least, we didn't relate it to anything in our favor. We had gotten the word that General MacArthur had been relieved of duty and some of the younger POWs had simply given up. The burial details were more frequent it seemed.

So, all things considered, we simply failed to relate any good with the fact that the Chinese were now encouraging us to take baths. Soon, we noted how the Chinese had us painting up our quarters, mopping, cutting down the trees, whitewashing the buildings, a bit of landscaping.

Rumors began to fly all over the place. First, the allies were knocking at the door. Next, peace talks were being considered. Finally, the rumor that we were going to be exchanged for enemy POWs. We began holding out for any hope. Ironically, the younger POWs stopped dying so fast. The burial details were becoming less frequent. "Hope is eternal," someone once said. No lie. I can attest to that. Give a man hope and he will withstand things he would never consider withstanding earlier when there was no hope.

Each day brought new rumors . . . new hope. Any stranger to the compound was noticed with special interest, especially if that stranger was dressed smartly and carried a briefcase.

I recall an incident near the end that I shall never forget. A group of us . . . Turks, Americans, South Koreans . . . were all on a work detail when the guards suddenly huddled around a stricken Turkish soldier.

They had pulled his pants down and had him lying on the ground face down. Two other Turkish soldiers were slowly, almost indifferently, pulling a tapeworm from his butt. The young Turkish lad never gave a whimper. It was as if he were getting a massage.

Quite frankly, I had heard about tapeworms all my life but in truth I had never really seen one of the things. On this particular day, however, I was to get an eyeful. One thing for damn sure, I had no idea they grew so long. The two Turkish soldiers seemed to be pulling his tapeworm for days, folding one end on the ground while more was being pulled out.

"Take care not to pull out any of his guts," I remember someone saying. I never looked around to see who made the remark. My eyes stayed glued on that Turks' butt and that forever long tapeworm. "What do you think?" one Turkish soldier calmly asked the other.

"I'd say so far we've pulled about twenty-three or twenty-four feet. Maybe a bit more. Who can tell?"

"Hurry up!" one of the guards shouted impatiently. "Gotta hurry up! Must get back to work. You take too long. Much too long! Either hurry up or cut off worm you have and leave the rest for later."

If looks could kill that little guard would have been killed tenfold because, to the man, everyone let go with one of those classic "I hate your ass" stares.

The two Turkish soldiers tried to quicken their pace. For the first time the lad on the ground appeared a bit anxious. A little sweat could now be seen.

"How you chaps doing up there?" he finally asked.

"Fine, m'boy. Just fine. A couple more yards should do it."

"Two minutes more. That's all! Two minutes more and we stop this!" The impatient little nervous guard again demanded. Again, the "stares of hate."

One of the Chinese guards lit up a cigarette. The way he struggled with the match, the ordeal with the tapeworm was getting to him much more than it was the Turkish soldier.

"Finally!" one of the two Turkish soldiers pulling the tapeworm shouted, "Finally!"

At that, they pulled the remainder of the tapeworm from the youngster's butt. The two took turns stomping on it. They then dug a little hole and buried it.

"Quite a worm you had up your ass, m'boy," one of the Turkish soldiers remarked. "Quite a worm."

"Quite an ass," the other Turkish soldier quipped. "Quite an ass indeed."

At that point the ranking Chinese non-commissioned officer stepped forward.

"Understand one thing comrades. He no get tapeworm here. It take years for worm to grow that long. That mean it started long before he got here. It grew on foreign soil. Not here!"

Who gives a damn! That was my first reaction to that little midget's remark.

"Now back to work! Move! Move!"

As we broke for work detail, the Chinese guard with the cigarette tossed it on the ground without bothering to put it out.

A white POW quickly scooped it up and began smoking it. Poppa Browne was nearby and glanced briefly at the black POWs present. We knew what he was thinking even though he didn't say a word. Didn't have to. He had said it enough for months.

> "Never stoop so low as to bow down and pick up a cigarette left by one of those people," he had warned us. "Never! It is

a disgrace to you personally and the entire race in particular. Now I know the white boys do it. Fine. They can get away with it. We can't. We have to be careful to hold onto our dignity when we can. Won't always be possible here. I know that more'n most. But we don't have to compromise on those cigarettes. We don't need those things to live. Don't ever let me see any one of you bending over pickin' up a cigarette tossed by one of those people. Never!"

This was a big thing to Poppa Browne. He preached this over and over again. Everyone complied. To have done otherwise would have brought down the wrath from the rest of the black POWs. We honored this request religiously. The Chinese took note of the blacks refusing to pick up cigarette butts and told our representative, Freddie Anderson, that we were very proud people, and demanded respect.

# 13
# Hank, From Back Home

While exercising outside our quarters, I was shocked to see my old boyhood classmate, Hank Williams. Shocked may be an understatement! Hank was my link to an earlier civilization. The times we once had, long before this nightmare.

"Hank! Hank! Hank!" I recall shouting, not knowing for sure it was he. Damn sure looked like him in the distance. "Hank! Hank Williams!"

He turned, paused in seeming disbelief, and ran over to me. That reunion was about as emotional as one might expect between two men in captivity who had not seen each other in years. Just to touch Hank was to touch living evidence that there was a "back home." When a person is confined in captivity for a long period, it becomes difficult to remember earlier realities. Fantasy sets in after a while. Disbelief. After awhile it appears as if you were never free. That all your previous life was nothing more than one great big fantasy. That your real reality was life as a captive. This is why it was so damn important to keep our mental focus. Poppa Browne would constantly drive this point home to us.

"Men, he would say, "no matter how difficult things get, always keep your focus. Never lose sight of reality. Failure to do this might mean a screwed up mind."

He never lied. It was so easy to lose sight of reality. So easy. This is why the sight of Hank was so important to both of us. It presented us with a much needed reference point! Damn! I was overjoyed at seeing my home boy.

Hank really looked well after the ordeal he had suffered. He had lost his toes during the winter march across Korea. He never mentioned it, however. Didn't have to. We talked a lot about home. About mutual friends. We talked long about our families. Hank was always in good spirits. We would see each other as often as possible. We re-established a very warm relationship during the next few months.

On one of my visits to the camp hospital, I was told that Hank had been admitted. I was worried and tried desperately to see him. However, I was unable to on that visit. Later, Hank asked to see me. I was called up to the hospital, not knowing what to expect. I had not seen Hank for several weeks during that time.

On this particular visit Hank confided that he had something he wanted his family to have. He really didn't look good at all. He looked weak and listless.

"Hank, you alright?" I remember asking. "You okay, buddy?"

"Sure. Sure." The man was not well and we both seemed to know it.

I tried to cheer him up. But, it was no use. We both knew what I was trying to do and why. Hank and I were too close for me to ever bullshit him. We both knew his days were numbered. I felt a little dampness swell in my eyes as Hank talked, whispered is more like it. At times I had difficulty hearing him.

"Tom," he began softly, old buddy, I want you to give this twenty-dollar bill and my ring to my family. This is very important to me, pal. If anything ever happens to me, please see that my family gets these, okay old buddy?"

I promised that if I were lucky enough to survive the place, one of my first visits on the outside would be to see his family, to deliver the items.

I went back to my quarters with these prized possessions of his. I hid them so that I could get to them whenever I needed to retrieve them.

I volunteered for hospital detail several times before the guards accepted my invitation. When you volunteered for something, the Commies thought you liked it and wanted to deny you anything that ever remotely represented a source of pleasure. I just wanted to check on Hank. When I eventually got the detail and visited the hospital, I was told that Hank had died. I brooded about his death for several weeks, more determined than ever to carry out my promise to him. I took his death hard, because his death meant a lost linkage to an earlier reality. I just felt empty.

During the next few months, several other fellow black POWs gave me items to give to their families. For some incredible reason, people seemed to think I was going to make it back when they weren't. I went along with their optimism, mainly because I really never doubted I would get back. I had vowed I would get back, in some form. I was not going to be buried by a bunch of Buddha heads atop some grassy hill in North Korea. Bullshit!

# 14
# Peace Talks Underway

The news hit us like a bombshell! Peace talks underway! A group of biggies from several nations were huddling in some place called Panmunjon. As far as we were concerned, they could have been having the damn talks in hell. We didn't care where they were holding them as long as they were being held.

The peace talks began about July 8, 1951 and dragged on and off until 1953.

To say that our mood changed is to state things mildly. We changed to the point of being a bit arrogant. We later found out that the peace discussions involved the Chinese, Korean and United Nations. Things looked serious. What's more, they looked damn good! We began to make preliminary mental plans, like what we were going to do upon return to the States. We had it all figured out mentally. What we had NOT figured out were the long delays during the peace talks. The many snags. Those days when word got back to us that the talks were not going well at all. That they may break off for good. Deep depression began to set in. We felt crushed! Drained! We had been on a mental high. Now, we were in the pits! I began to conclude that it would have been better if we had heard nothing until things were already settled. Dashed hopes for a man looking for freedom is extremely dangerous to his mental state.

Around Christmas 1951 our hopes were extremely high. The Communists and allied forces had at least agreed to exchange the names of persons each side had in captivity. This was a start. Perhaps this would pave the way for an actual exchange of prisoners. Everyone was happy with news of the agreement. I was to find out later that hundreds of families stateside stayed up quite late watching television hoping that names of loved ones would be announced. To be sure, there had been unofficial exchanges of letters. But, U.S. authorities had made it clear such exchanges were just that . . . unofficial! Quite frankly, the Chinese made it clear they were indifferent about exchanging names. They pointed out that all Chinese were busy fighting for the motherland and doing their best to stop American aggression. The mere exchanging of names to them were academic. Unfortunately, they found it difficult to understand the value we Americans placed on letting our families know we were still alive, although, in captivity. They found many contradictions in our lifestyles. They indicated that we grow grass only to cut it again . . . we loved dogs but hanged humans. We let dogs stay in homes but refused to sell homes to humans with dark skins.

As peace talks dragged on, we were allowed to take basketball and football teams on tours to other camps. (I should point out that I forever thank the Maker that the peace talks didn't end early as there would have been some confused people.)

As usual, the Black POWs were the stars, and the Chinese respected that. They would take some of the fellows out for special instructions. Willie was a good football player, he instituted a Rice Bowl. A goat was our mascot until it was needed for food. Willie puzzled the Chinese when he wanted to have skull practice at the blackboard; the Chinese would ask each other, "does the blackboard have any political value?"

Just after Christmas 1951, some officers and enlisted men

were brought up from Pyong-Yang where they had conducted a radio broadcast. Sergeant Fred Anderson informed Papa Browne that Major No-Field had told the Chinese if they had known of the conditions as they existed there, they would have put on a much stronger program, and they would like now to put on a program. The next morning Papa Browne met Major No-Field on the basketball court and told him, "I hear that you are planning on speaking to us today about making a recording?" Major No-Field said "yes," he wanted to speak to the fellows.

Papa Browne informed Major No-Field in no uncertain terms, "We have been getting along here very well without you officers and we want to keep it that way. Do you understand?"

"Yes," Major No-Field replied, I don't want to do anything that the men don't want. The Major returned to the Chinese and was heard to have said that he would not, under any circumstances, do what we didn't or the enlisted men didn't want or he would be eaten alive. This was the beginning of the complete separation of the ranks. Thanks to Papa Browne, the whole camp was indebted to him.

In August 1953, all NCOs . . . white and black . . . were moved to another location. We were placed on barges early one morning and traveled until around 10 p.m. that night. The only food given us was a red onion and a hot pepper. To this day I don't know whether those little bastards were trying to kill us or flush out our behinds. At any rate, that's all they gave us to eat.

Shortly after our move to the new location, markers identifying prison camps began to go up. Prior to that time there were no such markings. The Communists had emphasized to us privately that they simply didn't believe in going along with too much mandated by the Geneva Convention because they didn't believe in it. They claimed it was a capitalistic organization.

At the new location, "Bop Daddy" came to us and said an agreement had been reached to exchange all sick and wounded POWs. This news, too, was hailed as a significant development. It also proved to be another vehicle for those who were trying to

# True Colors

use every ploy to get released.

The exchange of the sick and wounded became commonly referred to as the "Little Switch." I guess this was so because no major exchanges were in effect at that time. This, to be exact, was in April 1953. "Little Switch" also became known as something else: as an opportunity for escape for some POWs who faked being wounded or being ill. To man's everlasting credit, he will use every opportunity to lie if this gives him a fair advantage over a situation. As child steals an apple from a friend's lunch box; a student peeks at his friend's test paper in quest of a better score; a woman lies about her age in an ever quest for youth, so, the art of lying prevails under normal circumstances. It is understandable that when a life and death situation arises lying is not only advisable but it becomes a much needed survival tactic.

So, when the sick and wounded were exchanged, many black and white POWs slipped back into the states under the cover of being sick or wounded. What's more, they got away with it.

To the black POWs, however, "Little Switch" became a disaster. They were subsequently accused, though not convicted, of being let through only because they had collaborated with the enemy. This was interesting because no such charges were leveled against the whites who slipped through, faking.

It is also interesting to note that, according to my research, not one of those blacks released during "Little Switch" ever completed their twenty years in service. Some were dishonorably discharged . . . others were discharged with something "less than honorable" . . . and others were subjected to such pressures that I conclude they simply decided to give military life up.

This is not to in anyway imply that all black POWs who came home by way of "Little Switch" were clean. I am certain, as explained earlier, that there were many who did their damn best to get out any way they could. I am only emphasizing that those who did get out this way appeared to have been "flagged" . . . sorted out for subsequent actions. This will be hard to prove.

However, there are many black former POWs still alive who will corroborate the latter statement.

To be sure, the U.S. Government did benefit from information given them by those POWs who returned via the sick and wounded path. U.S. Army intelligence reportedly received information as to locations of vital enemy supply points from the former POWs. Such information was helpful in subsequent allied raids on sections of North Korea. I would not like to go to my grave believing that only white POWs gave vital information. I would not like to believe this.

In May 1953, we were awakened early one morning by the sounds of sirens and the roar of planes, seemingly hundreds of planes. We had seen allied planes pass over before enroute to the enemy supply dump. But the numbers were nothing like this. This was most unusual. We didn't know what the hell to make of things. All of this unusual activity in the air was compounded by heightened activity in camp. Camp officials were seen hustling from one meeting to another. The guards, too, appeared on edge. The planes roared by all during the day and through the night. Although we didn't know what exactly was going on, we did respect the fact that they were allied planes. If nothing else, that was good.

# 15
# "Dig! You Dig Your Grave!"

I was standing in the doorway observing the planes early the next morning when two guards approached and demanded that I follow them. One gave me a shovel and commanded me to move out and fast! They kept grumbling to themselves. I didn't understand what they were saying, but I did conclude they were angry as all hell. Both had sidearms and rifles. They were serious!

"Dig! You did your grave!" one finally shouted in broken English when we approached a little hill overlooking the camp.

I nearly panicked!

"What for?" I remember asking nervously. "I haven't done anything!"

My question was met with a blistering slap across the face by the guard standing nearest me, not the one who gave the order to dig. I quickly started digging, then I suddenly slowed my pace, remembering that I had just been told to dig my grave. As frightened as I was, I was still rational enough to respect the fact that no man rushes to dig his own grave. No way! This was even more so when two angry people supervising the work were standing around you with loaded rifles and sidearms. Then, too, one had just slapped the hell out of me.

I was desperate! I thrust the shovel in the ground rhythmically, trying to prolong this job as long as possible, forever if I could.

"What did I do?" I asked loud and clear, hoping these people would understand me.

"Shut up!" came the terse reply. "You hurry! It's hot out here!"

I'm digging my grave and one guard was worrying about the weather. Nothing was making any kind of sense. I didn't recall provoking anyone. Why was I digging my grave? Why were these people angry with me on this particular morning? As I continued to slowly plunge the shovel in the ground, I couldn't help remembering how the Germans tried to bury their evidence shortly before the allied troops hit the concentration camps. Was I some type of threat to the Commies? Someone to be hidden?

I don't know how long it takes regular grave diggers to dig graves, but it took me the better part of nearly two hours, what with frequent rest periods and slow digging to draw this thing out. I don't know what I was hoping to happen. I was just hoping.

Finally, I reached the point where the guards were satisfied. They had long since taken seats under a nearby tree to shade themselves. From that position they would constantly yell at me to "Step it up!" I really wanted to step out of that hole and into their ass with my shovel but they were too far away. Again, I had resolved to do something rather than be shot like a damn loyal dog. The problem was, what could I do that made sense? That offered hope?

One guard approached the freshly dug grave while the other remained by the tree, his rifle trained on me. The guard who approached the grave had left his rifle near the tree, I guess for fear I might make a go for it. He took one end of the hole. Since the guard at the tree had his rifle trained on me there was little I could do without committing suicide and I knew it. The guard near me placed a blindfold on me and quickly hit me with his fist, slamming me to the ground backwards, but I didn't fall in the grave. I can honestly say I considered myself only seconds away from death. I experienced a strange feeling, not necessarily of fear, but one of complete numbness. All hope for surviving that ordeal had apparently left me with a resignation for death.

I remember struggling to my feet, expecting at best another blow and, at worst, a shot through the head. I didn't expect what actually happened.

When I finally regained my feet, one of the guards removed the blindfold while the other wiped away blood trickling from a cut at the corner of my mouth. Without saying a word, they led me back to my quarters. The walk back was very similar to a late evening stroll through a park. It was as if nothing had happened. No one ever explained to me the reasons for the actions against me on that morning. Until this very day the mystery remains.

In retrospect, I recognize that it was not at all necessary for me to understand the actions at the gravesite. I have long concluded that the actions against me at that gravesite were all part of some plan that was never disclosed to me. Still, I will always wonder.

A day after the allied planes completed their 24-hour aerial show, a group of POWs on wood detail came by the compound where we were quartered. When they saw us they began singing:

"Oooooo, yeah. The war'll soon be ovah! Oooooo, yeah. The war'll soon be ovah! Lemme hear ya again!"

"I say listen to me. The war'll soon be all ovah. Ovah! Ovah!"

Since the guards accompanying them could speak no English, the POWs were a little more energetic than usual in their singing. To be sure, they would, from time to time, strike into a song when marching to and from a detail. So, it was not uncommon for them to be singing their message to us on this morning.

"When did the old man say the war'll be ovah?" one of the POWs chanted.

"I tell ya he said 'bout midnight tonight," came a chanting response from another.

"I said the old man said this cock sucking war'll be ovah tonight. Tonight. Tonight!"

We understood the message but we didn't put too much stock in the reality of it, not at this time. Other than the unusual number of planes in the air the previous two days, there was very little indication to us that things were nearing an end. Sure, there were the rumors. But the rumors were always there. Rumor is a basic part of military life. Peace talks were on and off so we quickly lost confidence in their outcome.

In July 1953 a guard came for me and ordered me to a building in which I had been interrogated when I first came to the compound. When I entered, I was shocked to see a Communist Chinese general standing before me, casually smoking a custom made pipe. He was a scholarly type. Very friendly.

He spoke no English. We communicated entirely through an interpreter. He had before him what appeared to be a personnel folder. I couldn't be sure but I guessed it was mine.

The general was very calm throughout. He stated that I was obviously a leader . . . but that I seemed to have a knack for leading all the wrong causes. He said he figured I wanted to die but that they simply would not grant me the luxury. In a low-key lecture, he pointed out that in his opinion, based on all the evidence, I was simply a hot-headed person. He also took the occasion to state that he didn't hate any blacks, except perhaps one in the camp who gave every indication of wanting to be white.

"Just suppose, comrade," the interpreter relayed, "that I told you the war was over? Finished? Hostilities ended?"

With that statement it all came back. The wood detail singing their peculiar song. The unusually large number of planes. The more than edgy guards. The rash of meetings by camp brass. It was all so very clear now.

"Sorry, comrade, sir," I remember saying, "but I'm afraid I don't believe you. I've been through too much. I can't believe this."

# True Colors

How I wanted to believe it. Somehow I knew it was true . . . but somehow I mentally refused to believe that after all these months of hell it might all be drawing to an end. The general spoke to me about a half hour, mostly about my attitude, my reported arrogance and my failure to adhere totally to camp rules and regulations. I am sure the general expected me to deny all of the charges and I did.

On the way back to the compound quarters, the interrogator tried to convince me that if I would give them some kind of confession, in writing, they would stay off my back. He pointed out that if I didn't, there was always a chance that even though the war was ending, I could still be kept prisoner.

I thought about this for a day or so, concluding that they were going to come up with something anyway, so, perhaps I should at least control the magnitude of what they came up with regarding my conduct.

I decided to admit that I had violated some of the rules and regulations of the camp; that I had been in areas of the camp that perhaps I shouldn't have and I further stated that I found some camp regulations in direct conflict with my own government rules and regulations. I really considered all of this a bunch of expendable hogwash. But, it at least sounded good as a confession. I ended the so-called confession by being careful to state that it was my duty to disobey the enemy . . . this was one of the accepted rules of war.

The following day I was hauled into the main office again. This time there was no friendly general, only the interrogator. He was now acting in the capacity of judge. The minute I entered the office it was all business.

"Stand up straight and look ahead!" the interrogator commanded.

A day earlier this same interrogator was a mild mannered cuss. Now he was top dog with a vicious bite and I knew it. He lashed out with the traditional stuff, about our coming thousands of miles to kill innocent people, to destroy homes, to damage crops, to invade land of peaceful people and a lot of other nonsense.

I wasn't really concerned too much about what he was saying simply because I had heard it all before. However, I did take note when he rendered what amounted to a verdict:

"You all sentenced to two and a half years for your crimes against our people. You start your time only after war ends. Not before!"

I nearly crumbled! I only know I was shocked beyond belief. Everything seemed like a bad dream. Sometimes a tragedy is too tragic to be believable and to me, this was one of those times. There was absolutely no way for me to mentally survive two and a half additional years in that place. No way!

The interrogator looked at me and modified my sentence to one and a half years since I had confessed to my camp crimes. Even that didn't make any difference with me. I wanted to leave with the rest of the POWs, period! Not one day later!

The next day three of us were placed in a truck and transported away from Camp 5. During the journey, we were escorted by two trucks, one in front and one in the rear. Both contained members of Chinese rifle platoons. Prior to being moved out we were warned that if we made any noise or attempted to give any type signals we would be shot. The way the warning was given I had little reason to ever want to challenge it.

Along the way we passed groups of POWs, some crying, some shouting to us that they would tell folks back home what happened. Word had circulated quickly that we had been convicted of camp violations and would be kept behind.

The Commies finally took us to a place where we met other POWs who had been convicted of camp crimes of various natures. We weren't permitted to mingle with the other regular POWs. We were treated like celebrated war criminals. Eventually, there would be thirty-three of us who would be left behind as convicted POWs. I was to be the only black among them. We were also destined to be the very last POWs to leave North Korea.

Names of prisoners being considered for a POW exchange were being formulated. None of us who had been convicted would be eligible for any list in the foreseeable future! This had been made quite clear to us. I could write a hundred more pages about our mental depression and still not scratch the surface of how we actually felt. Who was it that said something like "these are the times that try men's souls . . . " Whoever the bastard was, he knew the score. We found ourselves calling upon all of our mental reserves. To be sure, some among us nearly broke several times. I guess, looking back, the thing that stood us in good stead was the fact that some official attention was now focused on us. We might not get back right away, but at least they couldn't screw around with us too much physically without affecting world reaction. I began to look at it another way. We were now some type of stars! Hell! If we were lucky, we might land in Hollywood! People might want to see and touch a real-life Korean tragedy. My fantasies were many. The mental exercises were mind strengthening. Good for stability. As one of the fellow POWs put it, "They need us alive as much as we want to be alive. They wouldn't dare put a foot in our ass now!" However, we were still captives, and still without any hope of early release.

Our ordeal became almost unbearable when the first group of POWs were exchanged. That was a big day for them and a mental disaster for the Forgotten 33, as we began to call ourselves. We had no idea at the time what type efforts were being expended on our behalf. There was, however, one thought that constantly nagged us: what would the government be willing to give up, if anything for us? One has to trust me when I say these thoughts at times were belabored. These thoughts, coupled with the unfairness of the mock trial, began to really play havoc with our mental state.

Tension began to take its toll among the Forgotten 33 as word circulated that the last of the regular POWs were exchanged. Several among our group began to cry, especially the youngsters. We took the departure of the last regular POWs quite hard. I felt sick! Once or twice I actually felt like vomiting. To this day I find it hard to relate my strange feelings on that day. God! I shall never forget that day. None of us ever will, I am sure. Took too much out of us.

The days slowly dragged into the weeks, the weeks slowly changing into months and still no sign of release for us, the Forgotten 33. In our minds we assured ourselves we were heroes. The world now knew we were being detained for being defiant! At least that part was driven home. We were being detained for being disruptive, for being unruly! For not going along with reported provisions of the Geneva Convention that called for us to comport ourselves like model prisoners. We were renegades! Sure! But we were proud renegades. Looking back at those who were held back, for the most part they were all men with singular minds. Outspoken, sure! But I don't think any of us were disruptive, in the purest sense of the word. This, too, I guess, is subject to interpretation. If trying to escape is being disruptive, then so be it. I never considered it was. It was my duty to escape if I could. At the time I did it, however, I was not necessarily trying to be patriotic. I was just trying to get out of a stinking miserable North Korean prison compound.

At times I concluded that we might spend additional years in that goddamn place. No one, it seemed then, was in a hurry to get us out. News about what was going on was suspect since we were getting it from the enemy.

Religion had always been a personal thing with me. To be sure, civilized man will always call upon some higher Being to deliver him through some great adversity. Our imprisonment in North Korea was no different. Black and white, Catholic and Jew, all found time to devote to their religious beliefs. Everything we did, of course, was makeshift. The enemy didn't take time to erect for us any temples or sanctuaries.

When the regular POWs left, religion really became a big thing for us. Maybe Willie had a point, maybe the Good Lord was the only thing in which we could truly believe. We found

# True Colors

ourselves huddling more with someone volunteering to lead in prayer. As I said earlier, black folk, especially black Baptists, could really pray. I put a lot of soul into praying. This is not to in any way make a mockery out of prayer, it's just that we are an emotional people. We pray and we tend to get excited when we pray. I got quite emotional in North Korea during those final trying days.

In those closing days, prayer became our constant companion. From it we got strength . . . faith in that which we could not see . . . hope from that which we could see, which was mostly ugly.

After what seemed like an eternity, we . . . the Forgotten 33 . . . were finally granted our release. It was all so very official, so procedural. Amazing! You spend agonizing months behind prison wire and your release is unceremonially wrapped in a sea of procedures. Our release, as expected, was also so very political. Both sides got their mileage from our agony. That's for damn sure!

Still, there was no great national fanfare. The newspapers moved the story. Television and radio did their usual news bit. But there were no tickertape parades. No one turned out to shower us with paper along Fifth Avenue. No intimate dinner with the President. No free tickets to the baseball games. None of that rah rah rah bullshit saved for later years. We were home. We were glad. Our families were happy. For those in the nation who cared, our nightmare had ended. For us, the nightmare would always be there. We would forever see the scars. The memory of those who failed to make it back would be a constant reminder. Hank Williams, in my memory, would never die.

As for the blacks who suffered under the Communists, it would appear that we cannot even endure pain at the hands of an enemy without someone saying we were either accustomed to pain, or that our agony was softened because we were a minority. As someone would remark years later, "being black can be a bit dangerous to one's health . . . No damn lie. So what else is new?"

I guess my own frustration is similar to that frustration shared later by veterans who got their tails blown off in Viet Nam, only to return home as outcasts for being there in the first place. There would be no ticker tape parades for them either and no lavish White House dinners, except for those Viet Nam veterans who were Nixon's guests near the end of Nixon's stay at the White House. No special tickets to baseball games. Just resentment from the very public they were trying to defend. It all gets so very political. So confusing and so unfair.

As I end this bloody story about Camp 5, I feel free now. I can now cast off chains that have been around my neck for nearly forty years. Still . . . there is another story to tell: the facts uncovering why many blacks unjustly accused of cavorting with the enemy . . . accusations based on unfounded charges and born out of questionable motives by one-sided courtmartial panels. Yes . . . unless someone else comes forth to tell it. I will have to delve into it, lest the chains around my hands stifle circulation to an already heavily overburdened brain.

I offer my own quiet TAPS for the guys from Camp 5 who did not survive to read their story in this documentary of North Korean hell. God Bless them.

## Afterword

There are hundreds of former black servicemen in this country living with the nightmarish stigma of once being accused of collaborating with the enemy. My own extensive research of World War II, the Korean Conflict and Vietnam has failed to produce one instance where a black serviceman was convicted of treason. But, documents will confirm that many have, indeed, been accused of treason. Like it or not, when a black in this country is merely accused of a significant crime, that is almost tantamount to a conviction. The stigma does the rest. Doesn't matter that a black soldier is subsequently freed of all charges, the fact that he was accused is often times enough to brand him for life.

Such has been the prevailing social system in this country.

In all candor, it is almost a cliche for me to be stating what everyone, white or black, has known for years. For decades, the black American fighting man . . . in the minds of the white military establishment . . . was looked upon as an inferior breed. In a report by the Army's Office of the Chief of Military History, it was pointed out that during World War II many white commanders, critically short on manpower, still refused to accept the offer of black replacements. The Army's study, authored by black professor D. Ulysses Lee of Morgan State College, documented the pressures exerted upon the Army to permit black servicemen to engage in major combat operations and not be relegated to traditional service units as cooks, truck drivers and mechanics. These pressures, according to the study, emanated from the black press, black leaders and the black community. I will always applaud these factions for their efforts.

The study went on to suggest that the lack of black officers during World War II and shortly afterwards could be linked to poor educational opportunities back home. Poor medical facilities also accounted for a high rate of physical disability among black servicemen. According to the study, in 1944 more than 58,800 black servicemen were discharged for physical and mental disqualifications. Keep in mind, all of these problems had "back home" roots. Add to this the fact that many states simply did not want black servicemen stationed in their areas.

In a word, the black serviceman came from a civilian society that attempted to relegate him to second class citizenship and into a military society that was staffed, for the most part, by white products of that civilian society. A uniform didn't necessarily change attitudes. In addition to all of the previously stated woes, the black fighting man also had to worry about an enemy from another country bent on blowing the guts out of anyone wearing an American uniform. That enemy didn't give a damn whether the man in an American uniform was white or black or driving a truck or tank. The enemy treated us all alike. They did not discriminate in their killing policies.

In Vietnam the black fighting man was in the forefront in terms of numbers. In that struggle they distinguished themselves at all levels. But, it is ironic that the Vietnam conflict will go down in history as the most unpopular war in which this country was ever engaged. The black fighting man as well as his white counterpart will never be remembered for heroics performed during that conflict. Nevertheless, that still does not diminish the significance of the heroics.

**The accounts in this book are based on incidents that occurred during my thirty-three months of confinement by the Communists. If nothing more, this work might keep alive the memory of agonies and injustices long heaped upon the black fighting man. They suffered and died hard in North Korea. To accuse any of them of unpatriotic acts is an insult to human decency.**

——James Thompson